Remember adversity builds character

Herm Vierano

FORTUITOUS MISFORTUNES

Thomas A. Viviano, Ph.D.

BALBOA.
PRESS

A DIVISION OF HAY HOUSE

Balboa Press books may be ordered through booksellers or by contacting:

Balboa Press
A Division of Hay House
1663 Liberty Drive
Bloomington, IN 47403
www.balboapress.com
1 (877) 407-4847

Because of the dynamic nature of the Internet, any web addresses or links contained in this book may have changed since publication and may no longer be valid. The views expressed in this work are solely those of the author and do not necessarily reflect the views of the publisher, and the publisher hereby disclaims any responsibility for them.

The author of this book does not dispense medical advice or prescribe the use of any technique as a form of treatment for physical, emotional, or medical problems without the advice of a physician, either directly or indirectly. The intent of the author is only to offer information of a general nature to help you in your quest for emotional and spiritual well-being. In the event you use any of the information in this book for yourself, which is your constitutional right, the author and the publisher assume no responsibility for your actions.

Any people depicted in stock imagery provided by Thinkstock are models, and such images are being used for illustrative purposes only.
Certain stock imagery © Thinkstock.

Printed in the United States of America.

ISBN: 978-1-4525-9747-8 (sc)
ISBN: 978-1-4525-9748-5 (e)

Balboa Press rev. date: 10/22/2014

Contents

Acknowledgments

I'd like to thank all the people with whom I've shaken hands who, while unbeknownst to them, became a mentor, a father, a mother, a friend, or a counselor.

Introduction

I was writing this introduction in my mind while on a hike with my best friend's dog Cookie, a two-year-old rescue that is part Chihuahua and part Jack Russell terrier. We were traversing a path at the Lehigh Gorge State Park near Jim Thorpe, Pennsylvania, and it was a slightly overcast day and cool for this time of August. Cookie looks at everything in awe and soaks in all of the new smells, sights, and experiences like a newborn baby. It is enviable and fun to look at things through her eyes. I am frequently outdoors, as I find places like these make me feel safe and unafraid. I imagine I spent most of my life grappling with some type of fear about something I had no control of. I always felt that nothing could hurt me out here in the bosom of nature, among God's most beautiful creations. I spent most of my life feeling alone, even though I was always surrounded by people who cared for me and loved me.

I spent a lifetime creating this concept of myself based on thoughts and emotions passing before me or based on what people told me I should do or who I should be. Michael Singer in his book *The Untethered Soul* asks, "Who are you that is lost and trying to build a concept of yourself in order to be found?" He goes on to say, "You will never find yourself in what you have built to define yourself." (Singer, 2007, p.

130) I had built this façade, this false persona, in order to have more control over my decision making and actions. I was not myself, but a collage of personalities, thoughts, emotions, and visions of what one should be like to be accepted, loved, valued, and successful, and fearless. The *Course in Miracles* states that "if you knew who walked beside you all of the time, you would never be scared." I was never enough, and until recently, was never really true to myself. I believe we all do have guardian angels, and in looking back over my life as presented in this book, it is a miracle that I am still here. Someone had to be looking out for me, and I imagine it was always someone from another dimension working though people here on earth.

When I wrote this book, it was with the intent of telling a few short stories and adding some comments about what I have learned through my own feelings and with reference to many modern psychologists, doctors, authors, and public renowned speakers in the field of self-help and life coaching. I've lived the last ten years of my life reading and studying Wayne Dyer, Deepak Chopra, Gary Zukav, Eckhard Tolle, Michael Singer, Cheryl Richardson, Louise Hay, and many others who have helped me make sense of my life and all of the good and bad that enveloped it. It seems that the more I learn and think I know, the more questions I have about everything. I am convinced that our development and learning don't stop here in this world with a physical experience, but continue in the nonphysical spiritual universe. There is an expression in education that learning should be a lifelong endeavor, but that saying should be taken further and reflect a learning that is infinite in nature. It is a type of learning that transcends the physical life. I believe we were given a physical component as one of many ways in which to grow. We needed to understand the power of the physical touch, smell, taste, and hearing in order to continue our growth in the next layer of existence, and use the essence of these senses to continue to construct what our spiritual self should represent.

I hope you enjoy reading about my life's journey to this point. As I look back, I have no regrets. Every stumbling block, every hurdle, every wonderful thing that has ever happened to me and every experience of adversity helped make me who I am today. You have a story too. Maybe it is somewhat like mine—or maybe completely different, but it's all worth telling and listening to. Tell your story so that others can learn from it and gain a better understanding of who you are.

Chapter 1

My Father

True fathering would be much more lacking than mothering.
Don't misunderstand me, both are needed—but the emphasis on
fathering is necessary because of the enormity of its absence.

—William Paul Young

House sparrows take about twelve days from hatching to fledging. As I watched the four baby sparrows flying around the little birdhouse that was built by students from a school where I worked, it was interesting to see the delight in their playful approach to their newfound skill. After only a day or two, it was sad for me to see that they no longer hovered around the small home in which they were hatched. The purpose of the house had been served and was no longer useful or needed. When I first brought it home, I placed it high upon a wooden swing set that I had built some twenty-two years ago for my three children. It took no time for the sparrows to discover it and make it the place where they would nest and hatch their babies. My daughter, Christina, would not let me take down the swing set even though she had long outgrown it. She is a traditionalist, and any change from her childhood memories saddens her. Somehow I don't think the baby sparrows would mind if anything happened to the birdhouse in which they hatched. Once pushed from the nest, their world became the open sky and the abundant trees. For some reason I hesitate to remove the structure from atop the swing set. Is there an underlying fear that if the sparrows returned, they would be saddened that the house no longer existed? Is it now an embedded part of the swing set that Christina forbids me to remove? Or could it stem from my own underlying fears of losing a home as a child? My father died when I was eleven, and my four sisters and I lived with my mother in our house for only a short time after. My mother had no working skills, so it wasn't long until my sisters were moved to foster homes and I ended up in a very well-to-do orphanage, the Milton Hershey School.

My parents owned a twin home on top of a hill in the outskirts of Pittsburgh that, by the time I was born into it in 1950, was rundown. It was a very high-maintenance, structured frame house made of wood and covered with old-fashioned shingles that were weathered and peeling off. The roof was in bad shape, and the windows had many layers of lead-based paint that you could see bubbling and peeling. There were fifty-two concrete steps overridden by beautiful rose bushes leading up to the front porch that my father had made. The porch furniture was also homemade from wood and was quite comfortable. My father was a self-taught and skilled carpenter but was old and losing his eyesight due to diabetes. We lived on a fixed income, so needless to say, we were a poor family in some ways, but in most ways I believe we were very wealthy. I thought in many ways we were better off than some of my friends' families in that our one and a half acres or so were full with fruit trees, grapevines, and colorful flowers. I used to pick roses and bouquet them for a neighbor's or friend's grandmother on the block, and they'd be so appreciative.

The property was bursting with various fruit trees, like green apple, peach, pear, and plum, with grapevines sprinkled throughout. The acreage was free from grass, and every foot of land was planted with either corn, rhubarb, tomatoes, peppers, green beans, radishes, cucumbers, or watermelon. In looking back, I don't know how my father found the time and vigor to work this land so arduously. This would have been difficult even for a younger man. What trees didn't harvest fruit were beautiful flowering trees, and in the spring you might have thought you entered the land of Oz. The bushes that yielded snowballs (Viburnum opulus) were also scattered throughout, and their fragrance was sensual and welcoming. There was a little sitting area that my dad made up on top of a small hill where I used to sit on early spring mornings and watch him water the vegetables and flowers and enjoy the sun shining through the hose water, which broke up the light into colors of the rainbow like a prism.

I had a sense that we were not well-off but didn't really understand that until I was told. Wouldn't it be wonderful if our positive self-perceptions were untampered with, unaltered, and uninfluenced by those who have the need to remind us of our misfortunes or define what they think our misfortunes might be? The fifties were a prosperous decade, and most of my friends and classmates had working fathers and stay-at-home leave-it-to-Beaver moms. I envied them so much. What I wanted was to be like them and to be what I considered normal. I think once I became old enough to be aware of my differences, I became overridden with shame and guilt. If I knew then what I know now, I would have realized how privileged I was.

I can remember being sent home from school in front of my classmates and being asked not to return until I bathed, combed my hair, and put on clean clothes. I returned that afternoon to school, and one of the students told the teacher to look at my pants and that they were the same ones I had on in the morning. In my defense, she announced to my classmate that I did wash, comb my hair, and change my shirt. Today, a teacher could be fired for sending a student home and embarrassing him in front of the class, but things were different then. All of this has helped make me who I am, and I appreciate these experiences now even though I didn't then.

My father was sixty-eight when I was born, and my mother was twenty-seven. He had five children from his first marriage; his first wife left him when the children were still young, and he raised them by himself. We therefore had five half-brothers and half-sisters who were really old enough to be our uncles and aunts. I can remember riding with one of my half-brothers and his wife to our dad's funeral, and he professed to his wife that his dad would still be alive if he didn't get married again and have those other kids. It was a terrible thing to hear—that your very existence was the cause of someone else's grief. I suppose that he didn't think I heard, but I'm sure a part of him wanted me to hear. I'm not sure I blamed him. Why did my father choose to marry again and have five more children at his age? It didn't seem like an intelligent thing to do. But if he hadn't, I would not be here, and I think now that my existence means something.

I think over the years I impacted others and made a difference in others' lives. And I think that's why we are here—to make something or someone better than it was before. We cannot change our past—it makes us who we are—but we can use it to make good decisions in the present and perhaps shape the future inasmuch as we have control. Lewis B. Smedes, a renowned Christian author and theologian, said, "Forgiving does not erase the bitter past. A healed memory is not a deleted memory. Instead, forgiving what we cannot forget creates a new way to remember. We change the memory of our past into a hope of our future." I've never tried to block out the memories of the past, even though some are painful, but I guess I did to an extent. I don't understand people who hide from their past. Everything you live through helps to make you the person you are now.

My father was a craftsman, a cabinetmaker if you will, and his favorite hobby was making acoustic guitars. He used two pieces of metal, made by one of his first sons at the steel mill where he worked in Pittsburgh, that were curved-cursive E shapes for the sides in which to mold the flexible water-soaked wood, a technique that is still used today by many guitar manufacturers. He trimmed the curved edges of the guitar with small trapezoidal shapes made from ham bones that were dried and hand cut. Sometimes every other one was painted black for effect. His weakness was his lack of ability to apply a professional finish to the instruments, probably due to his poor eyesight. His diabetes, which eventually took his sight and then his life, led to blindness and the eventual loss of his two legs.

My father with the instruments that he made

Richard Sennett in his book *The Craftsman* says "Craftwork focuses on objects in themselves and on impersonal practices; craftwork depends on curiosity; it tempers obsession; craftwork turns the craftsman outward." (Sennett, 2008, p. 288) I often use the phrase "getting lost in my work," as it is almost therapeutic and meditative; as I'm sure it was for my father. As I have done projects over my lifetime, I've come to know the pleasure of becoming involved in projects that require quality craftsmanship. I have failed miserably at some of them and have been successful at others. I enjoyed the deep connection that Sennett speaks about between material consciousness and ethical values. I think my father treated wood like it was a breathing and living entity as he molded it into furniture or a musical instrument. I can only imagine the joy he received in completing a stringed musical-instrument project and witnessed it come alive as he stroked it. It was his craftsmanship of these beautiful instruments that helped me to begin playing; I continue to play the guitar today.

I enjoy many hours of solitude playing and singing quietly for my own pleasure and always look forward to learning new songs. It is for me a form of meditation, a way of connecting with my father and a few others in my lifetime who enjoyed listening to me play and sing. I wish I had a better singing voice, but I learned from Karen Carpenter's song "*Sing,*" which says, "Don't worry that it's not good enough for anyone else to hear, just sing, sing a song." This allows me to at least tolerate my voice and enjoy the immense benefits that my music provides for my body and soul. I would watch my father play and sing Italian songs, particularly "*O Sole Mio.*" He often closed his eyes when he sang, and you could tell he was getting lost in the moment. This is the way I feel sometimes; what a wonderful gift my father has given me. As with most of us of the fifties, I first learned three chords—G, C, and D; with these you could play most of the popular songs of that day.

My father was a religious and very spiritual man, and occasionally took me to Mass at St. Stephens Catholic Church in our little borough of Hazelwood. I can't remember him taking my mother or any of my sisters to Mass. I was the only boy of his second marriage, right in the middle of four girls. Was this an old-fashioned Italian man who felt that men were the dominant gender and women should not participate in worldly events outside the home? I felt privileged but also a bit guilty. He had a temper and I felt that he lacked patience, particularly with us children. This could have been because of his age. My wife and I often said that we could not have raised our three children today at the age we currently are. It is a task that should fall upon the shoulders of youth. He swore, often in broken English, but never used the F word. One might say that he used clean foul language and very rarely crossed the obscene foul language barrier.

My dad was also very skilled in Italian culinary arts. His chicken cacciatore was out of this world, he made his own Sicilian-style pizza, he could present the seven fish at the holidays, which always seemed effortless for him to do, and the old standby pasta fagioli was a weekly staple at our house. He grew his own vegetable gardens, everything from corn to zucchini, and cooked mostly from his own creations. When he died, one could appreciate the loss. The gardens became overgrown and overridden by weeds. The roses and other beautiful floras were lost in knee-high unwanted vegetation, and this all represented a huge overall sense of a loss of the family patriarch.

It's funny what kids assume and take for granted. Every Christmas our grown children have expectations of the celebrations and traditions of holidays past. I always set up a train set, which was a cumbersome task; lately I set them up but didn't plug them in. I don't think anyone noticed. All they cared about was that they are out and on display. I think it's devastating for these traditions to be cut off from you at a young age. Traditions are just that, and when you have no ownership in the decision to discontinue a tradition, you feel like you lost something and it was beyond your control. We all should be allowed some control, some decision-making power, to feel valued.

My dad was the ultimate protector. Something about my personality invited bullying when I was in school. It's as if I gave off an odor or an aura that attracted the bullies. I don't think it was the poor dress or hygiene, although I would suppose that was the initial trigger. I think they could sense my fear. I don't know if this is something you are born with or something you develop as a result of your environment. Nature versus nurture, so to speak. I can remember him getting dressed, putting on his hat, grabbing his cane, and escorting me to school to speak to the principal. Here we are some fifty-five years later and parents still do this. You wonder why the education system has not changed over that time. Each time I interview a student about his victimization, I wonder what personality attribute he has to attract this attention. Nonetheless, it was nice to have an advocate, and the bullying did stop for a while after each episode.

I thought my dad died a terrible death with the onset of diabetes. First he had a toe amputated, then his leg at the knee, then the other leg, and he ended up legally blind. It was my job to roll his wheelchair into a bathroom that was put in for him by one of his sons-in-law. I would take him in, help him with his pants, and then transfer him from the chair onto the toilet. This must have been so hard for this man who was so active and self-sufficient even throughout his senior years with gardening and other work around the house. I often wonder now how I would be if inflicted with a disease that stopped me from playing tennis, running, biking, and doing all the things that make life enjoyable for me. Although I use my mind for work, I rely so much on my body for exercise and fun outdoor activities. It is said, however, that the mind and body are one. Every part of our body has intelligence and is connected to thoughtful decision making. It's this universal consciousness that can help heal ourselves with meditation and other forms of self-awareness.

After my father died that July in 1961, my protector was gone. My mother had the same fear inside of her as I had, so there was no defender there. Our neighborhood at one time was an all-white working-class Pittsburgh steel mill town east of downtown, but it slowly turned into an all-black neighborhood, though I'm not sure why. I suspect that in those days when one black family moved in, it created a scare, a chain reaction resulted, and slowly the neighborhood changed over. For the most part, my new neighbors were very nice people, and my new friends were mostly all black. Like all kids we sometimes had our differences, and one weekend I had words with a couple of the kids from a safe distance so I felt bold enough to stand up for myself. I remember kids saying that they were going to beat me up after school one day, and I asked my mother to meet me at school to escort me home. She never showed. I felt abandoned on so many levels. In hindsight, the slapping and hitting didn't seem so bad compared to the helpless feeling that maybe no one cared. When I arrived home crying and asked why she didn't come, I got no response. There was no hug, no comforting, and no words of wisdom. I felt alone, but now I think she did the best she knew how.

Chapter 2

My Mother

*A mother is not a person to lean on, but a
person to make leaning unnecessary.*
—Dorothy Canfield Fisher

I do believe my mother did the best she could. I don't know what I or my mother was thinking this night I am about to describe to you, but in retrospect, it was one of the most imprudent actions of my life. It was around midnight during my holiday break from Milton Hershey School when I awakened to banging on the front door. I was thirteen years old. I came downstairs and advised that we not open the door. There was silence for a short time, and then we heard banging on the outside basement door, through which they gained access. I immediately went to the kitchen and drew a knife from one of the kitchen drawers and stood by the first-floor basement entrance door, which led into the living room. I could feel myself shaking as the intruders made their way up the basement steps. They began to pound on the basement entrance door until it was flung open in front of me and my mother.

There were two adult Caucasian males, who entered as if they were invited guests. The looks on their faces when they saw the knife were of amusement, as they knew I was helpless against their adult strength. "Look," said one of the men, "you'd be better off with a gun, as anyone could easily take the knife from you and use it against you." This came off as a bit of fatherly advice if you will. These men knew my mother. In fact, these men knew my mother intimately, as I found out later. My mother prostituted herself and my two older sisters to make money. Later on people told me that there was an article in one of the Pittsburgh papers regarding a woman who was arrested for prostitution, and her children, four girls, were taken away from her.

I remember that day that she called me at the orphanage crying that she was being arrested and that the girls were being taken from her. I felt so helpless. I didn't know what to tell her to do but to call one of my father's firstborn children to seek help, but realistically I didn't think anything would help at this point. By this time the two families were estranged; it was just a shot in the dark.

Anyway, the rest of that night we just sat and talked (they talked and I listened). They were primarily trying to convince me that since I went to an all-boys' school, I should extort money for homosexual favors. They said there were bound to be boys there that were gay and that I should take advantage of this. It amazed me how right on they were, but I would never think of this myself. Was I that much of a prude? I always felt that if you were on the receiving end of a gay person's actions, it made you a gay person yourself. The stigma of a gay person in those days was very negative and implied either poor choice or a disease of some kind. I finally went to bed, and I assume the two men let themselves out without incident. It seemed as though they were just looking for a place to hang out and have a couple of beers—at least for this night.

My mother was a very short, skinny woman; when she dressed up, she might have been considered somewhat attractive. I always felt that she wore too much makeup, but I guess that's how women wore it in those days. Our house was filthy. Whenever I brought home a friend from school, my friend would make fun of the dirt and disorder that surrounded us. They never wanted to come back. Since my father was legally blind most of my life to this point, I guess he didn't notice it. We had white venetian blinds that were almost black, vinyl floors that were sticky and cold to the touch of bare feet, and furniture with holes in it. The toilets were often un-flushed, and baby portable toilets sat in the bathtub waiting for someone to empty them. I can remember one of my half brothers going to the bathroom on one of his visits to my father and dragging me upstairs to empty one of the portable toilets. He was very angry, and I guess looking back, he really wanted to say something to my mother but found it easier to tell me.

My mother had no religious convictions. She never went to church nor did she encourage her children to go. We went to public schools, but our father insisted that we go to catechism. After our first year, my two older sisters and I made communion. We went back for a second year to begin the confirmation process. I studied very hard, and I connected well with the nun who taught us. Often we would exchange holy cards or religious trinkets. I have forgotten her name but will never forget her influence. At the end of the year, we were told that we could not make confirmation then as it was a two-year process. The sister said that it was a shame as I had worked so hard. It was over that summer that my father died, and when we went back for the second year to continue our studies, we had a different nun, who turned out to be one who seemed to lack emotional intelligence and sensitivity. To put it in kids' terms, she was a mean nun. She never seemed to utter a kind word of encouragement and just had a terrible disposition. With no parental figure to encourage me to go, I stopped going, and my sisters did whatever I did. They were not going to go without me.

To this day I have not been confirmed and feel badly about this. My wife encouraged me to pursue this, but I have no desire to do that. I continue to be a casual Catholic at best, and while I enjoy Mass, I do not attend or practice devoutly. It's not a matter of not believing, as I believe there is a greater source from which we emanate and of which we are still a part, but I like to embrace all religions and exercise wonderment in learning some of their thoughts, philosophies, and beliefs. John Denver said to his wife in the movie *Oh God,* where George Burns played God, that God doesn't believe in religion. I am a firm believer in this, as I don't understand why God would embrace one belief system over another.

It seems my mother had little regard for us children. It wasn't unusual for her to slap us in the face in order to discipline us, which of course breaks a child's spirit. She could turn a smile into a tear instantly. I had little or no respect for her and pretty much began to do what I wanted. Her word of authority meant nothing. When my father died, I knew there was insurance money left over after funeral expenses. All my friends had bikes and I wanted one in the worst way. In hindsight this may have been very selfish, but I was a kid. Also, I felt a parent might think that it would help a grieving child if he received a gift from his father's inheritance. I ended up finding an old bike frame in the woods. It had a rear rim on it with no tire and no wheel at all in the front. I ended up cutting down a thick limb to use as an axle and used a wagon wheel that I found in the woods as the front tire. It looked hideous, but I took it up one of our hills in the backyard and rode it down as it had no pedals on it either. I had hours of fun with it, but was embarrassed when one of my friends came over unexpectedly and caught me riding it. I ride a bike today and love it. I bought a $500 Gary Fisher and am very proud of this bike.

I used to accompany a friend of mine on his paper route, and then afterward didn't get home until two or three in the morning. I wasn't doing much of anything during this time but walking the streets and talking to others kids that were out late as well. I was out of control. I stopped going to school and missed most of my sixth-grade year. A guidance counselor there arranged for me to visit the all-boys' orphanage, in which I eventually enrolled sometime in July of my eleventh year. It was the most beautiful place I'd ever seen. It was located in central Pennsylvania, and it had beautiful rolling green hills and scattered student homes, which were worth then a quarter million dollars. Each student home had a set of house parents, and usually fourteen boys stayed at each home. We were two to a bedroom with modern furniture and what I thought were luxuries that I had never enjoyed before. My worries were over. Food, clothing, and education were abundantly provided. It was my way out. My sisters never got this kind of opportunity. Back then, this school only accepted boys, but this changed in the early 1980s. I wish my sisters could have had the same opportunities.

I used to think when I was home that I chose the wrong group of kids to hang out with, but in looking back, my desire to be accepted, liked, and secure made me the undesirable one to be around. I stole from my mother's purse to buy things for my friends or myself, and didn't realize I was taking necessities from my family. My thin skin of civility was slowly continuing to erode, and I was only thinking of myself. I can remember being beaten mercilessly with a stick and my mother yelling, "Stay away from those kids!" If she only knew that I was the corrupt one. I was the one who badly influenced all those others that she told me to avoid.

I do remember one day when my little sister was crying that she was hungry, I took her out back to one of our peach trees, put some salt on an unripe peach, and gave it to her. It gave me some satisfaction that I was thinking of someone else for a change.

One Christmas my mother sent me ten dollars for Christmas shopping. My housemother took us out to the department store, and I bought gifts for my sisters and my mother. We bought some great gifts and got a lot for ten dollars. There were baby-dolls for the little ones, and makeup mirrors and such for my older sisters. They were delighted and surprised when I brought them home, and I really wish I could have made a tradition of this.

The next Christmas I was fourteen and had a girlfriend. When I received the ten dollars this time, I bought my girlfriend a sweater and brought home nothing for my family. How selfish was I? What they must have thought of me! Why was providing gifts my responsibility, though, I began to rationalize. Aren't parents supposed to provide Christmases for their children? And where were the gifts from the extended family that we used to get when my father was alive? They were very generous to us. When we were little, we each received five gifts since there were five older half siblings. This ended when my dad died.

I imagine the disappointment I felt that first Christmas without gifts was the same disappointment my sisters felt when I came home from the boys' school empty-handed. Why could I not anticipate their feelings from my own disappointed experience? I often hear of young boys who take on adult roles in their father's absence. Why couldn't I have been that person?

My father, mother, me, and my sister Maryann

I walked into the kitchen one evening to get something to eat. On top of the cabinet that came up to my chest was where we kept the loaves of Wonder bread. When I approached the bread, I stood there eye to eye with one of the biggest rats I'd ever seen perched upon the loaf of bread. I think he was as frightened as I was. He didn't move, and it seemed like we stared at each other for a long time. I slowly backed away and warned everyone not to eat the bread. After that we got a cat. I think someone was giving away kittens, so I grabbed one that had a beautiful tan, white, and black coat. I didn't know how to treat a pet as I was never taught how to. I was abusive to him, and I think he finally died of malnutrition and abuse.

My mother rolled her own cigarettes, as many did in those days I presume, and also bought them by the carton on occasion. There was no research about secondhand smoke or smoking during pregnancy in those days, so whatever afflictions one could get from such an environment, I'm sure we sustained. I tried smoking myself while at home for a while but didn't like it. Here again, it was an acceptance thing with friends;

I became popular by stealing them a pack at a time so she wouldn't realize they were gone. I suppose it made us feel like adults or big shots.

One time when I was home on vacation from the boys' home, I asked my mother for a cigarette and she let me have one. Our differences seemed to mellow at this point as we saw each other so infrequently. Often when I came home, there was very little food, so I encouraged my mother to go to the store and ask the manager for food on credit. I didn't go with her because of the embarrassment, but was surprised to see her and one of my sisters coming up the street with bags full of groceries. Why did she feel compelled to listen to a fourteen-year-old? What kind of power and influence did I have with her that sent her out on this venture? Was it her need to have a male figure in her life from whom she could take direction? Maybe she always wanted to do this but needed affirmation from what she presumed to be the stronger gender. It must have been hard trying to raise five kids without a male figure around. In those days, it was considered a dysfunctional family not to have both parents in a household, as opposed to it being the norm of today. It was still the Father-Knows-Best era. I still believe that she did the best that she could.

Chapter 3

My Sisters

Your siblings are the only people in the world who know what it's like to have been brought up the way you were.

—Betsy Cohen

They say that civility in a young boy is quickly eroded without the presence of a father. I found that there is nothing more true. I was standing at the top of the staircase that led from our back bedroom to the kitchen holding a juice glass. I stood there waiting until my older sister Virginia reached the bottom of the stairs, and then I let the glass go. It struck her on the head and she began to cry. God, that must have hurt. Why didn't I think that then? She was in her early teens then and very fragile. We always thought that she would be a secretary, as she always was doing paperwork. She used to keep a list of the top one hundred songs on the radio. Songs from Elvis Presley, the Everly Brothers, and Pat Boone were very popular then. She was very shy, soft-spoken, and considerate, and I imagined that others would have considered her pretty. She was in special education classes, but I think this was more due to her introversion and quiet nature.

She died when she was twenty-five and I was about twenty. I was in the service then, and a call was put out to me from my staff sergeant; he called me in and gave me the news. I was issued a weeklong leave and went home to pay my respects. She died of a heart attack. I guess she was violated so much that she lived in a constant state of fear, anxiety, and insecurity. I can remember a relative saying to me, "She is better off." How are you better off dead at twenty-five? Was this supposed to comfort me? She never experienced the wonderful things that a little girl, a teenager, or a young woman should have experienced. She never went to a prom and was never held by a man who loved her. She would never experience marriage, the joy of sex, and the bliss of having children. This all was allowed to be taken from her by her mother, someone who was supposed to protect her and make her feel beautiful.

My sister Virginia

I could only imagine what those nights were like being abused by older men and being raped in the true sense of the word. Who does this? Who takes advantage of a young girl, unwilling to participate, scared, and so vulnerable? Today these men would be in jail. I don't know who did it, but I thank God someone stepped up and called the children and youth services. All four girls were taken out of an environment that wasn't fit for animals.

Maryann told me they never got to her. She must have been strong-willed. She was a year older than I, and while our two younger sisters were lucky enough to be placed in foster homes, no one wanted an older teenager. So she spent the last few years of her teens in a state school and hospital outside of Pittsburgh. She was educated there, fed, and clothed, and learned life skills such as home economics. Although she had a big heart, she was an unattractive person. Her eyes were somewhat crossed, and she had the features of a person with Down syndrome but was never diagnosed as such. Before she left Hazelwood, she too was in special education classes at Gladstone Elementary School. She lacked reasoning skills and did not have good reading, writing, and math ability.

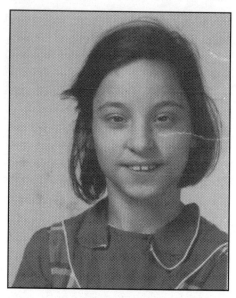

My sister Maryann

As adults, I took a picture of Maryann once with a Polaroid camera, and she took it from me and tore it up. She knew she was unattractive, and I felt so badly for her. At the same time, I felt ashamed when I was younger when I was with her in public. In retrospect, I was such a weak person. I lacked the bravery and nerve to be proud of her. I cared too much about what strangers thought. I cared about what my wife and kids thought as well. I don't think I gave my spouse and children enough credit. I knew many people with retarded children or siblings, and they didn't seem to be ashamed of them. Why did I feel this way? As I became older, I got over this, but in many ways it was too late. Maryann died in her fifties of cancer—far too young. I should have taken her to Disney World, camping, the beach—anywhere to get her out of Pittsburgh for a while. I brought her to my house in Philly on occasion, and she seemed to really enjoy that. Sometimes she expected to come for a week in summer, and again I disappointed.

My heart breaks when I think I was not there with her when she died. I visited her a few days before when she was in terrible pain, and I knew she didn't have much time but I left anyway. Our cousin, who lived in the bottom apartment, found her dead in her favorite chair and called me with the news. For some reason, Maryann had a $5,000 insurance policy and wanted to be buried in a cemetery with dignity. She left everything out on the table. Of my three sisters who died, she was the only one who planned for this. For one who I thought was the least intelligent of us all, she out-planned everyone. She even said that she wanted a headstone, so I saved enough of the insurance money from the modest burial to buy a stone a year after her death, waiting to make sure the ground was settled. We buried her a few yards from our father, and on the rare occasions that I visit the cemetery, I visit them both.

I guess Theresa was about four years old when we were celebrating our traditional Christmas Eve gathering, and she, her cousin Lou Ann of about her same age, and I were standing together as guests were arriving. Lou Ann was dressed impeccably. She was wearing a beautiful chiffon dress with white stockings and a pair of shiny black patent leather shoes. She looked like an angel. In contrast, Theresa had on one of my dirty white T-shirts that came down below her knees as though she were wearing it like a sack dress. Her brown hair was messy, and she had no shoes on. When one of our uncles came in, he gravitated toward Lou Ann, lifted her up over his head, and asked, "How is my precious niece doing?" Theresa was standing by giggling in anticipation of being picked up next, but he only bent down and asked, "And how are you?" I felt an enormous embarrassment for her, and I could see the disappointment in her face. I don't remember receiving any greeting from him, but I don't remember being bothered by this.

Carmella, my youngest sibling, lost her battle to cancer in February 2012. She was a lifetime smoker, and even though I often suggested she go through a smoking cessation process, it was impossible for her to quit. Never being a smoker, I don't pretend to understand this, but I have a great regard for those who have found a way to quit. She was divorced from her husband after a few years and has a child from this marriage. They lived in a small sort of a detached in-law house that was provided by her husband's sister in Glassport, Pennsylvania, a small town outside of Pittsburgh. I remember Carmella feeling controlled by her husband and his family; she always seemed to be unhappy. She used to waitress in this little town, and before that I remember her having dreams of working in the allied health fields.

I don't remember much about her childhood as she was very young when I went away to the boys' home. I remember her being a very beautiful child, the only child in our family to have blond hair and blue eyes. She called me one day and asked if I could help her move out of her bungalow after her husband left her. I went back to Pittsburgh that weekend with our minivan, and after three trips, had her moved into her new home that she was going to rent. She was very proud of this home as it was the first time she lived on her own with her daughter Chris. Before her daughter was eighteen, there was always a threat that her Chris's aunt would take her away from Carmella. There was always this perception I believe by her in laws that if Chris were with Carmella, she would not get the education and work ethic she needed to be self-sufficient. I remember Carmella carrying this fear well after her daughter turned eighteen. After Carmella died, her daughter did end up moving in with her aunt, even though she was a young adult.

Chapter 4

Me

Don't walk behind me; I might not lead. Don't walk in front of me; I may not follow. Just walk beside me and be my friend.

—Albert Camus

Me at age eight

'll never forget the spring Sunday back in 1964 when my housemates and I were walking back to our student home from church on the long, serpentine driveway that threaded around each student home when we saw a 1963 Mercury Monterey pull up beside us. To my surprise, it was my half brother Joe and his family, who decided to take a Sunday drive to see me as they heard I was enrolled in Milton Hershey School. It was about an hour and a half drive from their Levittown home in suburban Philadelphia. That day I would begin a relationship with Joe and his family that I still enjoy today.

Joe and his wife, Doris, have since left us, but their children and grandchildren remain close to my heart. From that point on, they treated me like one of their family. They welcomed me into their home when we were allowed to leave school on occasions such as over the Christmas, Easter, and summer holidays. I felt badly for not going home to my mother's house in Pittsburgh, but I knew I would have a better time with Joe and his family and would not be a burden on my mother and four sisters.

Joe's home was small, but I was able to fit in nicely by sharing a bed with his oldest son, Frankie, who was a year older than I. The house had four bedrooms and one bathroom, a small kitchen, and a comfortable living room. It was shared by Joe, Doris, and their four children: Frank, Terry, Bobby, and Barbara. I felt so comfortable that I even became annoying at times and almost took it for granted and assumed that I was one of five children. No one ever complained, however, as this is how they wanted me to feel. It felt so normal to be considered a part of this family, and I welcomed this normality immensely.

Milton Hershey was great, but I don't think anything beats the traditional American family. We ate together every night family-style, and Doris was a great cook. I wanted to add this piece of my life to this writing because I feel that they had a great influence on me and gave me a foundation and basis for what a family should look like. It helped form my family belief systems and hopefully helped me somewhat in the raising of my three children.

On the first series of downs after our opponents had the football first, the ball was fumbled on the exchange between the center and me. It was my first start at quarterback that 1968 season, and that's not how I wanted to begin the game. I recovered my own fumble, and after that incident, the exchanges were smooth and second-nature. We were in control the whole game. Our running game was unstoppable, and just about every member of the backfield scored a touchdown. How we lost the game was unfathomable. We led 19-0 until the middle of the fourth quarter. We were on the opponents' five-yard line and were about to score again. Since the coach let the quarterback call his own plays, I called a quick out pass to one of our running backs. I threw it too gingerly, and it was bobbled and intercepted in the end zone. From there the opponents scored three unanswered touchdowns with points afterward and won the game twenty-one to nineteen. We were stunned. What or who was to blame? The interception? The defense? The coach? We outclassed the other team the whole game. I defined myself by that interception for a long time. How many people did I let down?

We went on to win only one game that season—our homecoming game. The coach started our regular quarterback but had me take over halfway into the first quarter. I had a good passing day, but the defense had a spectacular outing, holding the opponents to six points. We won seven to six. Our extra point failed on our only touchdown, but because of a penalty, we had an opportunity to try again. Our coach called for a fake field goal and I was to pass the football into the end zone. In those days there was no such thing as a two-point conversion. My friend Jim, the placekicker, reminded me that I had to make sure as soon as the ball was snapped that I as the holder got off my knee so the ball was not downed. I executed the play perfectly and threw a routine pass right down the middle to a running back, which gave us a seven-to-nothing lead. The other team scored but failed on the extra point attempt, and we left the victors.

*Me standing on top of Milton Hershey's senior
hall overlooking the football stadium*

This helped to alleviate some of the embarrassment from the interception of a previous game, but it was still haunting. We as humans are hard on ourselves. We hate to let others down, at least those of us who still retain a need to please people to some degree. To this day I am a people pleaser, but I have started to realize that you have to please yourself as well. You cannot discount yourself by dismissing your own needs in service to others' needs. People don't really want this.

I was eleven when I arrived at Milton Hershey. My elementary school counselor recommended this school to me and my mother, and he made it sound so inviting. They had farms with animals, top-rate education, and everything was free. What he didn't mention was the excellent discipline structure. In the end, this became the most valuable asset to me. There were fourteen of us at a student home with houseparents. We were up at five-thirty every morning, got dressed, and did our chores. Half of us went out to the barn to milk the cows, and the other half stayed in and prepared breakfast. My first job was to wash the cows' tails so that when they wagged them, nothing dirty would get into the milk. You had to hold onto the tail tightly while you washed it; otherwise it would whip you in the face, and nothing hurts more than a wet-tail slap to the face. I also scraped the barnyard of cow manure and did all of the other menial tasks until I was promoted to actually milking. The hardest non-milking job was carrying the heavy milk buckets into the milk house and dumping them into the large pasteurizing machine. The house duties were not as laborious, but not as fun either. There was vacuuming, dusting, cleaning bathrooms, washing dishes and pots and pans for sixteen people, and cooking breakfast.

At the time I didn't realize the value of all of this. I think it gave me a strong work ethic and helped me with time management. With all of this, we had to get our homework done and reserve time for leisure activities such as touch football, basketball, baseball, and soccer. We had student home teams in all of those sports and competed against each other through to championships. It taught us about teamwork and the value of healthy competition.

Milton Hershey School not only saved my life, but made me realize that there was a quality of life well beyond that in which I grew up. It gave me back my pride in schoolwork and pride in knowing what I could accomplish academically. Due to my previous homelife, I missed most of my sixth-grade school year because I had cut so much. One might say that I fell into the educationally disadvantaged group, in which you come from a culture or community that does not value education. School was not a safe place for me, so I missed as much as I could. I left every morning but came back home and either told my mother that they sent me home sick or I would just hide in our backyard until the end of the school day. My mother never called the school to check to see why I was sick, what I was sick from, or just to see if I was lying. I spent some cold and lonely days outside either on our roof or out in the large backyard. It was the colder days that I said I was sick because I didn't want to spend the day outside.

The school and truant officers finally contacted my mother and she had to go to court. She told me that they wanted to fine her, but when she broke down and cried in front of the judge, he exercised leniency and she had to promise she would get me to school. She did get me to finally go back, and it was very humiliating. Silence fell over the class as I entered the room, and it looked like the teacher was notified and prepared, but my classmates were not. Today, there is a whole reentry procedure to make this process as comfortable as possible for the returning student, as it is normal today to see a student return either from an illness or from being detained or incarcerated for one reason or another. I continued to cut but not as often, and this was when the intervention occurred from the guidance counselor.

Once I found out that I would soon transfer to the MHS, or the home as it became known to me, I was comfortable missing the rest of the year, and my mother seemed to accept that this was going to be until I left. What a relief to her this must have been—to finally be rid of me and not have to worry about my truancy and other bad behaviors that defined who I was. She could then concentrate on the four girls, but this didn't go well either for her or for my four siblings.

When I arrived at Milton Hershey, the first thing I wanted to do was go for a swim in the student-home pond. There was a float out in the middle made of a wood platform supported by four big metal barrels. Once I changed into a bathing suit, I stood there at the edge while my mother and my new housemother watched and encouraged me to go in. But I never went in; I think I was too afraid. It wasn't until later when other boys went in that I joined them, as I felt secure knowing there were other kids in the water. I think I always approached life this way to a certain age.

I think I learned early in my young adulthood that I should make my own way. Without parental guidance and their participation in an event, it's pretty difficult to try something new. If I wanted my child to go into the water, I went into the water first. I couldn't imagine my child doing something that I didn't do myself. I think this provides for a secure and safe childhood. It's these parenting skills that are handed down from generation to generation that I may have missed. I remember teaching my boys when they were young how to shag fly balls before they went out for the Little League teams so that they could be prepared. I remember trying out for a Little League team when I was eleven, and they put me in center field. The first ball came down and hit me in the chest. I think the second one came down and hit me in the chin first and then hit me in the chest again. I never went back. I don't think I knew at the time what advantages the other kids had by throwing with their dads. I just thought I was unskilled and should stay away from that sport.

My first experience with basketball was a cardboard box that I hung up in the hallway of our house; I used a milk carton as the ball. I enjoyed this. I think sometimes that children's activities are overregulated. I could entertain myself for hours when I wasn't playing with other children. My favorite was playing a cowboy. I could play forever with a cowboy gun and a holster. I could be the sheriff one day, the bad guy the next, or could play the Lone Ranger. I don't think anyone had an imagination such as mine. This was, of course, out of necessity.

One time in the home I got into trouble, as I let myself into the houseparent's quarters and stole a model tractor that was sitting on one of their coffee tables. Since it was a farming community, it wasn't unusual for people to have such decorations in their homes. I played with it for a while but then returned it. I must have put it back in the wrong spot or on a different table, because they knew somehow it was tampered with and our whole unit got into trouble. I was asked multiple times as I was new, but I denied taking it and the attention over it soon died. I didn't think that I really did something wrong, but it was the reaction of the house parents that made me feel that it was criminal and I was scared to death to admit taking and playing with the model tractor. I was just using my imagination as I always had to entertain myself. In thinking about this today, had I admitted to this act and explained my intentions, they probably would have understood. Fear ruled my reaction here, as it did for a lot of my life.

As it turned out—but I wasn't real sure about this then—I ended up being a good-looking, young, athletic teenager, and became popular. I modeled myself after some peers and became quiet and unassuming when I realized how popular they were. They oozed with self-confidence, and I was determined to be like this although this wasn't truly what I wanted to become. I suppressed a more outgoing personality, but whatever made me popular was fine with me at the time. A quarterback should be an outgoing leader type to gain the confidence of his teammates. I just considered myself one of the players who held another position on the team.

This worked up until my junior year, as the coach called all of the plays. We got a new coach in my senior year, however, and he allowed the quarterbacks to call their own plays. He even taught us how to call an audible with the magic color of the day. Each position player had a number along with each gap on the line. The quarterback was one, and each of the other backs had ascending numbers. The slots on either side of the center were one and two, and either side of the guards between them and the tackles were slots three and four. So a typical play could be a two-number description of where the play would take place. If the quarterback called a thirty-three, then the number three back would run through the number three hole between the guard and tackle on the left side. The odd number slots were on the left side, and the even numbers were on the right side. However, if the play-call was a thirty-three and the quarterback saw a huge opening up the middle, he could audible and run a quarterback sneak. If the magic color was blue, the call at the line of scrimmage then would be defining the defense, the magic color, and then the new number. As the quarterback aligned under the center, he could say, five-man line, blue, eleven, and repeat.

The new coach came from a semipro team, so he didn't realize that this approach may have been too much for a high school team. This was a lot of responsibility on the quarterback, the running backs, and the line, as there was perhaps too much communication occurring before the play, which may have confused players at this level. This type of play calling required a strong leader at the helm, and this may have been one of my weaknesses. The coach leader perhaps gave his player leader too much responsibility.

It's ironic that I am an educational leader today and truly believe that the best leaders bring out the leadership quality in people that they lead. I feel that the people that I lead should be given the freedom to think, and their leader should find value in this. Those being led should be able to express confidence in independent thought and have opportunities to implement their ideas, and the leader should encourage the sharing, discussion, and debate of all of their input. Those who we lead need to know that they can make mistakes with relative impunity, that they can lash out in a moment of turmoil and mayhem and be forgiven, that they can express their ideas and have them listened to, and that they can be empowered to make decisions that they feel will benefit all. They need to know that they have leaders who not only hold them accountable, but are compassionate and live in harmony with fairness, justice, honesty, trustworthiness, and loyalty. My coach may have been ahead of his time.

Some say leaders are born, not made, but I am not sure I agree with this. I certainly was not born into a family of leaders, nor did I ever feel this was natural to me. What was natural to me was listening and helping people make their own decisions. I believe 75 percent of leadership is listening, 5 percent is advising, and 20 percent is helping people arrive at their own resolution. Almost everyone has the drive to do his or her job well and succeed. It is our job as leaders to foster this desire and recognize when it comes to fruition. Lao-tzu in the *Tao Te Ching* describes leadership as follows:

With the greatest leaders above them,
People barely know one exists.
Next comes one whom they love and praise.
Next comes one whom they fear.
Next comes one whom they despise and defy.
When a leader trusts on one,
No one trusts him.
The great leader speaks little.
He never speaks carelessly.
He works without self-interest
And leaves no trace.
When all is finished, the people say,
"We did it ourselves."
(quoted in Dyer, 2007, p. 76)

Chapter 5

My Early Adult Years

Adulthood brings with it the pernicious illusion of control, perhaps even depends on it. I mean the mirage of dominion over our own life that allows us to feel like adults, for we associate maturity with autonomy, the sovereign right to determine what is going to happen to us next.

—Juan Gabriel Vasquez

graduated from Milton Hershey School in 1968, worked over the summer at U.S. Steel, and attended community college that fall. I didn't thrive in community college; after barely two years, I dropped out. I don't know if it was all of the freedom or the self-responsibility of getting the work done, but it was all overwhelming. I think a large part of it was the social dynamic. I came from an all-boys' home, so I was terrified of girls. But it was the large population as a whole that I think led to my early demise. I was horrible at interacting with people, and I think that part of this was the new personality I adopted of being quiet in Milton Hershey School. That worked in the home, but in the real world, you have to be assertive and social to be successful. As a result of this personality I adopted, people never really got to know the real me. The only people that did get to know me well were girlfriends, and they used to say if people knew the real me, they would like me. I guess I came off as aloof, self-centered, and at times uncaring.

After I left community college, I took on all types of jobs, none of which I liked. I didn't qualify for anything that I would like, especially without a college degree. In those days, a college degree meant more. The quality of the job you got and the compensation were really commensurate with your educational background. We all know that's not true today. Even though most jobs today require some type of postsecondary experience, it's not necessarily a four-year degree. Most employers today look for an applied skill, usually obtained through a certification, which can be obtained through a community or junior college or through a career and technical center for high-school-aged students. I had no concentrated experience, so I undertook work in factories and department stores; these jobs were low-paying and very dull. There was no opportunity to use creativity or problem-solving skills, which is the lifeblood of self-satisfaction in the workplace.

It didn't take long for the military to realize I no longer qualified for the college military exemption, so I received my draft notice in June 1970. I couldn't believe this. I barely had my freedom from being in Milton Hershey, and here again I would be bound by a system where I had no control. I actually don't think it was the fear of going to Vietnam; rather, it was not having control over my own destiny. I had a girlfriend at the time and just wanted to be with her. I felt so disoriented, confused, and angry. I couldn't figure out why this was happening to me.

I reported for my physical and was in perfect health. After my physical, I received my reporting date and arrived at the Philadelphia Induction Center with hundreds of other draftees. I guess I knew this was going to happen if I left college, as I had a very low number in the draft lottery. We were sitting around the television during my senior year watching the draft lottery by birthday, and March 16 came up around the number sixty-seven. Out of a possibility of 365, this was pretty low.

I often wonder how many young men died because of this arbitrary number. A number drawn out of a rotating barrel determined your future, or if you would have much of one. This is why college deferments were so popular. I believe, however, that this college generation eventually ended the war by being the allies and advocates of young men in the military during the Vietnam era. They could have been just content with the deferment, but instead, they protested against the war, which I believe enhanced the decision to eventually pull out of Vietnam in 1975. They fought here at home for the poor and uneducated, who represented the majority of young men who went overseas. I think young Americans lost this drive to foster change like this. We're one of the few countries where people are content to let government make decisions for us.

The young men of the Vietnam era didn't have the respect and honor that came with the uniform in preceding wars. We were spat upon by citizens who may have lost a son or another loved one. There was little honor in that uniform during that era. All we did was do what we were told, and yet we were being held accountable for a war we had nothing to do with. We thought we were being as noble as those who served in World War II or Korea. It was a time of confusion of loyalty to country and countrymen. It was no one's fault; it was just young boys doing what they thought was right.

I ended up at Fort Dix, New Jersey, that summer for basic training, and it was hot as hell. If it was over ninety degrees, we were allowed to roll up the long sleeves on our fatigues. We force-marched in the deep sand, and it made us feel like you weren't getting anywhere. Tempers were flaring in the ranks during these force-march exercises, and to make things worse, you weren't allowed to drink from your canteen until we broke for a rest. This all made sense, as they were preparing you for Vietnam, but it seemed cruel. I can remember a solder marching behind me who took out his canteen and splashed water on the back of my neck. It felt so good, and I appreciated the risk he took. He could have been in a lot of trouble. He was a friend and a humanitarian.

I ended up losing so much weight and my body resistance went down so much that I ended up with pneumonia and was hospitalized for about a week. I had a lot of catching up to do, and there was a risk of having to repeat boot camp if you didn't score well on the Physical Training (PT) test at the end of training. I ended up passing but didn't score as well as I would have liked as I was still weak. We had to run a mile in less than seven minutes and normally this was my strength, but since it was the last of five events, I was too exhausted to beat that mark.

Kitchen Police, or KP as it was referred to, was the worst. You had to report by 4:00 a.m., and it wasn't done until nine o'clock that night after dinner trays, pots, and pans were washed and put away, and everything else was cleaned. What was so exhausting about this was that you still had to make revelry the next morning at 5:00 a.m. The verbal abuse was unbelievable. The cooks and the servers yelled at you the whole time and were demeaning; they knew the right words to use to make you feel insignificant. Once I was commanded to pick up a dirt pile in the middle of the floor. The cook pointed at it with his foot and yelled for me to pick it up. This was tricky because if I walked away to get a dustpan and brush, he would have yelled at me for walking away from him. If I bent down to pick it up, he would yell at me to get a dustpan and brush. It was a lose-lose situation for me. I chose to bend down and pick it up and was correct in my prediction. He was all over me for not using a dustpan and brush, and the fact that I was down low to the ground and he was standing made it even a more demeaning event.

I understood well the intention of my NCOs to make it tough on us so that we became battle-tough, but there were just certain circumstances when I felt that people were taking advantage of this philosophy and making it more difficult than it had to be. The fact is that soldiers had to eat. So the preparation and cleaning were done out of necessity, not out of training, especially since we were not training to be cooks or servers, but training for the infantry. This was abuse beyond purpose and reason.

At this time in the sixties, there was also a black revolution going on, and it infiltrated into the ranks of basic training. I had two fights during my tenure in the military, and they both were with black men. It was my experience in my two years of service to have many black friends. In fact, I toured most of Italy with a black peer. He was from California, and we had a ball touring together. In some instances, though, there were run-ins with young black men not wanting to perform certain duties that we all had to perform just because they thought they were getting picked on for racial reasons.

One day during a forced march, a black soldier refused to take his turn being a road guard. A road guard was chosen each time we began our marches; the guard needed to wear a yellow vest and run ahead into the street where we crossed to hold up traffic. When this particular person was asked, he refused. When the squad leader tried to put the vest on him, he resisted and wanted to fight. Before anything further ensued, another soldier stepped up and agreed to take the position. I hope the resistant soldier was reprimanded for this. This is the part of training that I believe is rational and important, as in battle, you don't want to let your squad down and you must carry your weight. You have to remember that these were impressionable young kids, who probably had difficulty distinguishing between what the right thing to do for the team and when to stand up for their own rights.

In one incident that I was directly involved in, it was about two o'clock in the morning. We were trying to sleep, and a young soldier who had been drinking was walking around from room to room with a nightstick beating on the beds and yelling. I got up and went to the charge of quarters sergeant (CQ) and let him know what was going on. He did nothing to intervene. The perpetrator returned, and when I got up to report him again, he grabbed my arm. Instinctively I turned and punched him in the jaw, and we broke into a skirmish. He was a strong little guy, and he eventually ended up on top of me on the floor; the CQ arrived and pulled him off me.

In another incident, I was walking down a busy hall when an African American and I bumped shoulders. We both stopped and turned around, and he said, "Watch where you're going." Without thinking I said, "Fuck you." I was wrong here. I wish I could have reversed that and said sorry or excuse me, but it was too late. He came to my barracks later that afternoon when I was napping on my bunk, and he stood over me and asked, "Do you remember me?" Before I knew it, he had his heel in my face with a powerful kick, and I was no match for him. A friend of mine pulled him off of me. We ended up shaking hands, and I apologized for my words.

These were angry young men. The majority of the young men who ended up going to Vietnam were poor and uneducated. They ended up bearing the brunt of the Vietnam war—white and black alike—and there was huge resentment. Protecting our country does fall upon the shoulders of our youth unfortunately, because they are strong, impressionable, and take orders well. It just wasn't fair that so many of these young people lost their lives for a cause that no one believed in. They didn't go to Canada or go AWOL, but stood and served when no one else cared.

For my advanced individual training (AIT), I ended up at Fort Belvoir, Virginia, where I studied electrical and generation theory in preparation to supply electrical power to mobile army surgical hospital (MASH) units. This is frontline duty, but I did as well as I could in order to gain rank at the end of each phase of classes. I was relatively intelligent, and the army had great schools and instructors. Money was no object, and the equipment was second to none. I ended up a specialist fourth class at the end of my advanced training, which is equivalent to a sergeant. I wanted to do this to earn more money. I was prudent and purchased bonds with this money; I sent the bonds home to have them banked.

For some reason, when my orders came for my permanent assignment, I was being sent to Livorno, Italy. I had figured out my budget for going to Vietnam, where you could get extra pay for being stationed in a combat zone. I wasn't disappointed, but I never expected this. My buddies were mostly going to Vietnam, and I felt badly. I also felt a little badly about having a higher rank than those who were coming back from Vietnam wounded. I thought those guys should have been gaining rank simply by having to go there.

I ended up going to Italy in January, when the temperature at Livorno ranges from forty to fifty degrees and it rains a lot of the time. It was very beautiful there, and I got used to the place pretty quickly. My job ended up being a generation technician, and we supplied uninterrupted power to a strategic communications facility. Their job was to provide missile information to Italy, and since European power was 220 volts and 50 cycles per second, it was our job to convert the power to 120 volt, 60 cycles per second, since the American equipment operated on these values. It was an eight o'clock to four thirty job, and except for the occasional extra duty, I was off during the evening.

I was able to purchase a used car and a new motorcycle with the money that I saved from liquor and cigarette rations, as well as my regular salary. Since I didn't smoke, I was able to sell my rations to others who did. The same went for liquor. The car was a boxy-looking Fiat that needed some work, but the motorcycle was a brand-new 125cc Beta off-road vehicle. It had large knobby tires to navigate through all types of terrain, but I wanted more of a hybrid or road bike to tour some of Italy. I took the bike back to where I bought it and had them put on some street tires that gave me a smoother ride and weren't as slippery in the rain. I was able to tour some of Italy on this bike and got to appreciate the hilly, scenic countryside. I ended up losing control of the bike a couple of times on wet roads and took some minor spills that I was able to recover from quickly with just some bruises and scrapes. I thought the bike was beautiful. The chrome was shiny, and the tank was a nice-looking metal-flake green. I was very proud, even though by most bikers' standards the bike was very small and meant for trails.

I had one what I thought to be serious accident on the bike, and it rendered the bike undrivable. I was on my way to work one morning doing about forty kilometers an hour when a car pulled out from a stop sign and I ran into his front bumper. It was unavoidable. I guess the driver just didn't see me. This was before the headlight law came into effect for motorcycles. I felt myself flying through the air, and when I landed, I felt my head bounce off the pavement a few times. This made me a firm believer in helmets; I'm sure this may have saved my life. Excruciating pain, however, came from my shins; I must have hit the handlebars with them as I was ejected and flung forward from the impact. I was sure at least one of my legs was broken and can remember yelling out in pain. I also remember being consoled by the passenger of the car, an older Italian lady who cradled my head in her arms as I lay there weeping. What I remember most vividly, though, was looking up and seeing the driver of the vehicle back up out of the intersection and go behind the stop sign. I'm not sure if this was an attempt to protect himself and set up a scenario that looked like I ran into him versus him running a stop sign or if he just wanted to remove his car from harm's way in the middle of the road.

The ambulance came, and there was a huge crew at the hospital waiting for me; they must have radioed ahead to be ready for anything. As I entered the hospital, the pain seem to subside, and miraculously there was nothing broken. I remember feeling a bit guilty about all the attention I was getting for what turned out to be minor injuries. One of my shins did swell, and I was on bed rest for a few days. It was as though someone took a sledgehammer to my shins; I can't imagine what a broken shinbone would feel like if what I suffered was just severe bruising.

It turned out that the driver of the vehicle that pulled out was a colonel in the Italian army, and he was afraid of some fallout and repercussions with the US occupancy there, but the dignitaries got together and were able to work things out. After I left Italy, I was able to have the bike shipped home by a friend. I rode it for a while here in the states but tried to do as much off-road stuff as I could to remain safe.

I was getting close to fulfilling my two-year commitment when I received a call from my staff sergeant that I needed to come down to see him. He informed me that my twenty-five-year-old sister Virginia had died and directed me on how to get a pass to go home. Since I was so close to the end of my tour, I was honorably discharged and didn't have to go back to Italy. I gave a friend of mine power of attorney to ship my motorcycle home for me.

My sister's death was going to change my life, as death always has a way of making us appreciate the real meaning of life—at least for a while. Death shocks us and we slow down, reflect, and take a close look at the meaningless tasks we perform every day and the petty things that really make us nuts. As useless as we might think these actions are sometimes, I believe they are a built-in safety mechanism. If you think how miserable we all would be if we never got over someone's death, we can see that God's plan is that we get lost in the mundane everyday tasks that keep our minds from things that really depress us. It's all a reminder that life is for the living.

I left the service in January 1972 and took a position as an electrical apprentice in local union 98 of the IBEW of Philadelphia. I was accepted before I was drafted into the military but could not get exempted or get credit for the service unless I had six months in the business, so I had to start from scratch at age twenty-two. My half brother Joe had sponsored me, as in those days you practically had to know someone to get in.

My experiences were good and bad, but mostly good I suppose. As an apprentice, you are at the low end of the chain, and just being out of the service, where I achieved the rank of specialist fifth class when my tour was complete, I was used to being in charge sometimes. The money was good, however, so I did what I had to do to make it through the apprenticeship and get along with everyone. We attended class one day a week where we learned electrical theory, and the other four days were on-the-job training. I thought that being involved in wiring some of the Philadelphia skyline high-rises was a great experience: you got to see things that the other working citizens of the city didn't get to see. It was neat to be on the roof of a fifty-five-story building on a windy day and feel the building swaying. The sights from up there were spectacular as well.

These were well-read and well-rounded journeymen who had a plethora of experiences to talk about. They were well-paid and many had invested wisely in shore homes or the market. Many had boats and were avid fishermen. I found that they were also well-versed in politics as well, especially those involving labor and the labor unions of the city. One aspect of the business that I didn't like was the picket lines. I felt uncomfortable standing in front of a building while others were crossing the picket lines. I thought how they needed to make a living and had families too. Pennsylvania is not a right-to-work state, so any government jobs had to pay prevailing wages as established by the unions. I always thought that there was enough work for everyone and that the smaller mom-and-pop electrical contractors should have a right to bid jobs as well. One thing that the unions could sell was craftsmanship. We were trained and educated well to do our jobs, and that justified our salaries. Not every contractor gives its employees proper training in the crafts, and a lot of it was on-the-job training.

The recession of the mid- to late 1970s hit, and a lot of us were out of work for a while. It was my first experience being laid off, and it hit me hard. This was around the time I met my wife. I was collecting unemployment and playing in a top forty band to help me get by. I met her at a nightclub called the Townhouse in northeast Philly. I was out with a few of my buddies from the union, and she was out celebrating her nursing degree with some friends. I thought she was inebriated. She had a very high energy level, was dancing and laughing, and was fun to be around. It turns out she didn't drink. This was her personality. She was very vivacious and lively, and was just celebrating her recent graduation from St. Agnes Hospital in South Philadelphia with a few friends. I don't remember who the other two girls were, but after we were married, she never spent much time with them.

We were married about a year and a half later and rented an apartment in northeast Philadelphia. It was a small second-story apartment with a living room, kitchen, bedroom, and bathroom. It was fun watching her decorate it with a powder-blue carpet and curtains to match. We struggled our first year. I imagine it was like any other first year of marriage as you get to know each other's nuances and idiosyncrasies. You truly don't know someone until you live with them. I can't even remember what we fought about, but we made it through the first year and things seemed to settle down.

The band helped me live out my fantasy as a rock star. Sometimes you receive an amazing high and chill from performing a song that was done perfectly and received well by the spectators. There's no thrill like it. I can't imagine what the big rock stars must feel like, and I can understand the addiction of the high you get performing live in front of tens of thousands of people. The famous French-American artist Marcel Duchamp said that "the creative art is not performed by the artist alone; the spectators bring the work in contact with the external world by deciphering and interpreting its inner qualification and thus adds their contribution to the creative act."

I started off just wanting to be part of a small folk group doing Simon and Garfunkel material and the like. I couldn't find anyone willing to just do this as there was no money in this. Everyone wanted to play the clubs, and this required performing top forty numbers. After trying out for some already existing bands and mixing with some who wanted to start a new band, I was able to get a foursome together. We had a bass player, a drummer who did lead vocals, a lead guitarist, and me, who played rhythm guitar and did some vocals. We were bad when we started out. It takes a long time to get to know each other's styles, and emotions would run out of control. Most of the time we got along all right, but I think every one of us quit at least once and returned.

I used to wonder why the popular groups like the Beatles and others broke up when they seemed to be doing so well, but after being in only a part-time band, I quickly learned why. You travel together, sometimes stay at motels overnight together, you get to know each other's families, and all of your vulnerabilities are exposed. A modern social work researcher, Brene' Brown, studied shame and vulnerability, and she said that "you truly cannot become connected with another human being until you expose your vulnerabilities." (Brown, June, 2010) Otherwise, your relationships are based on superficial and shallow dialogue. The more you hide or suppress your vulnerabilities, the more vulnerabilities you have. This can only last so long in a relationship, whether it be a band, a marriage, a business partnership, or whatever; sooner or later your vulnerabilities surface. In the end this is a good thing; as you begin to work past these, your relationships develop more deeply and are more meaningful.

Chapter 6

Adversity

When something bad happens to good people, follow them—for they are angels from whom we can learn.

—Thomas Viviano

So why would it be necessary to share these stories, one might ask? Many people have grown up in more devastating backgrounds than mine. Some children grew up being physically, sexually, or verbally abused, neglected, handicapped, surrounded by mental illness or alcoholism, or in a criminal environment generated by their parents. Some grew up in third-world countries enduring poverty with very little food, water, clothing, and shelter. Some grew up embedded in an environment impoverished by war.

More common stories are the ones like mine, which a lot of times will create embarrassment and humiliation rather than rendering one a hero or one who has overcome a monumental adversity. To us, however, these adversities are monumental no matter what time of our lives they occur. Some people grow up and live lives unscathed by misfortune until they are older and lose a family member or go through a divorce. It may be even harder for a mature adult to handle these types of losses, as he or she has gone on for so long living an unharmed existence. A child, on the other hand, may be more resilient by nature and because of a lack of experience and a short duration of time with a loved one, is more capable of recovery; at least this is how I view my experience.

I truly believe that adversity makes us who we are. I don't think we truly look at ourselves and what we are made of until some misfortune has crossed our path. One who has never been through adversity has never been tested for character in a way that only hardship can test. There are many who believe that we chose earth before we were born and chose a direction that was full of challenges because of a predetermined need to grow, learn, and find out what we are truly capable of.

Jean Houston in her book *The Wizard of Us* proclaims that "we can help ourselves by reframing the traditional road of trials that every hero must endure in the hero's journey by turning it into a road of adventures filled with opportunities for growth rather than attacks from outside of ourselves. We are not victims. Adversity is not something that a superior, cruel, unseen force is doing to us. We are active creators in our life experiences. Unfortunate pitfalls or misplaced steps along our yellow brick road are in fact opportunities to learn who we really are and what we are capable of. All encounters in our life have been divinely orchestrated by us in order to assist us in our growth as human beings on earth and the expansion of our souls." (Houston, 2012, p. 151)

If we believe this, then we believe people choose a life of starvation or abuse, but who knows why. It could be out of sympathy or empathy for a relative or friend from a previous existence. It could be a way of easing our own guilt for having witnessed others who have gone through this in a former life.

In her article in *Education Weekly*, Bonnie Benard speaks to the resiliency of youth who were exposed to adversity and how a large percentage of these youth become healthy and competent young adults. The research says there are four attributes that youth possess that allows them the resilience to overcome adversity: social competence, problem-solving skills, autonomy, and a sense of purpose and future—or basically hope. If I could share a story for each one of these attributes, it might give one a better understanding of how these traits are useful.

Social Competence

At the orphanage that I attended, it was a ritual for the school president to invite new students to his house for dinner and a get-to-know-you evening. I found this to be extremely generous and a kind gesture and was so appreciative. I was a little nervous going there, but I knew that there would be other boys there in my same situation and found comfort in this. As it turns out, the president was very easy to talk to and personable, which allowed us to feel comfortable in conversation and social exchange. We retired from the dinner table to the living room, where dessert was served to us. Even though there was a server, after dessert I insisted on collecting everyone's dessert plates and cups.

I ended up dropping a spoon on their beautiful rug, but the president made an excuse for me that I was just trying to be helpful. The bottom line here is that I felt socially competent enough to do this, although it may have been considered bad judgment to help clean up. I think that it is this instinct that helped me survive in what I may have considered a childhood filled with adversity.

Problem-Solving Skills

I was in advanced individual training in Fort Belvoir, Virginia, where I studied generator operation and repair for servicing mobile army surgical hospital (MASH) units. It was the last day of training, and orders were given to assume your permanent post where you would serve in what you were trained to do. My orders came down for Livorno, Italy, but the information and logistics were incomplete and vague at best. The officer in charge didn't know quite what to do with me but asked me to stand behind him until he got to me. It had been my experience to this point that if officers were not quite sure what to do with you, this probably meant some busywork duty until they could investigate the details of my assignment. I also knew from experience that this could take a long time due to military bureaucratic procedure, and I wasn't about to get caught up in that.

I therefore took the paperwork that I did have, sketchy as it might be, and made my way to the offices where these assignments were generated. I went right up to the first clerk that I saw and asked him what I could do to complete this reassignment process. He handed it off to someone who handed it off to someone else, and after some paper stamping and signatures, I had all the information I needed to move on to my next post in Europe. The people in that office were actually appreciative of my assertiveness, as they wanted this off their plate as well.

I never ran into that officer in charge again, and that was certainly fine with me. By the time he delegated and finished cutting orders with all of the other troops, I'm sure he forgot about my presence anyway. So adopting this plan of action while I was in the presence of the officer and resourcefulness from others were very critical here.

Autonomy

Webster defines autonomy as "the state of existing or acting separately from others." I felt that in many situations it was by necessity that I did this. In my high school years, it wasn't uncommon for fellow students and friends to sneak away and smoke or drink, but I somehow resisted this peer pressure to do what my friends were doing. The same held true when I was in the service, in the band, or in college and work situations. I had an inner advisor and mentor that told me what was right and wrong, harmful to my body, or immoral. This self-regulation helped me throughout my life to listen to advice, internalize and analyze it, and make decisions autonomously. It's not that I never made bad decisions, but I was able to own those mistakes—because those are the only things we truly own—and learn and grow from them. I find that the key to life is to live autonomously, but within the context of others' advice and mentorship, and have the wisdom to choose and filter through all of it and decide which advice I should take.

A Sense of Purpose

In her book *The Wizard of Us,* Jean Houston relates the three supporting attributes that we all have in us but may fail to develop over the years. Courage, wisdom, and heart are characteristics that our three characters seek from the infamous wizard, and it's through their journey to seek help that they discover they had these virtues all along. The scarecrow in his search for wisdom, which he thinks he would have if he had a physical brain, discovers that ironically having the ability to want a brain is in itself a thought process that requires intelligence. Through their dangerous journey, he develops and cultivates ideas on how to escape or attack. The lion shows bravery in the face of fear and adversity, and in effect, this is how bravery is really measured. It's acting in the face of fear, not acting in the absence of it, that truly defines bravery. The tin man in his quest for a heart shows that he already possesses one in his compassion for his fellow travelers throughout their mission. In the end, Dorothy discovers that she needn't look any farther than in her backyard to find what she is looking for. For her, it was not about having what you want, but about discovering how to want what you already have.

There is a hero in every one of us; you don't have to slay dragons or conquer countries to be a hero. Other characteristics of heroism include self-knowledge, healthy coping skills, strong interpersonal and personal life, and a personal and purposeful meaning of life.

Chapter 7

Divorce

*Some people think that it's holding on that makes
one strong; sometimes it's letting go.*

—Sylvia Robinson

It was I who requested to separate and divorce my wife of thirty-six years. I had a sense that we were becoming detached, aloof, and uninterested in each other. Maybe it was never right. Maybe we did the things we were supposed to do because we were both ready, but I can only speak for myself. You couldn't ask for a better spouse if it were a good fit. She is a very attractive, caring, and giving person, and I'm sure all of my male friends and acquaintances are wondering what I was thinking. I've been called a lucky bastard many times by male greeters and of course they were right. On the surface that's the way I should have felt. But it goes way deeper than this. Given my background, I think I was looking for a caretaker, maybe the mother I never had. It is said that we are all treated the way we ask people to treat us, whether intentionally or subliminally. What I asked for and what I needed years ago no longer holds true today. Unfortunately, in an effort to change myself and to discard all that was in me that I deemed unfavorable, I had to discard the very person that I dragged into my life as part of what I thought I needed. What my wife had represented was all of my dependency on another person to make myself whole, to deem myself worthy, to help boost my self-esteem, to help keep me safe. In the end, I was unhappy.

I think what made me forge ahead was hearing a psychologist speak about her experiences while interviewing people on their deathbeds. When asked what regrets they had in their lives and what they would go back and change, the number one answer was they would live more for themselves and less for someone else. They sacrificed their lives and happiness for children or husbands or wives, and in the end, made very little difference for those that would have benefited from this kind of sacrifice. The best thing we can do for others is to be happy with ourselves. Sacrificing for others so that they may be happy may leave an empty feeling inside the beneficiaries that creates a lack of fulfillment, or even indifference because maybe they really never knew that these sacrifices were being made. The sacrifice leads to high expectations on the part of the giver and eventually leads to great disappointment in the form of what he or she was doing being unappreciated. Staying in a marriage for your children where you are unhappy is a good example of this type of self-sacrifice.

Dr. Christiane Northrup, a renowned medical expert, speaker, and author, says that the best gift we can give our children or anyone else is our own happiness. Children and other so-called victims of a divorce should frame their experience as positive. If they claim that divorce devastated them, it inevitably will. All will come around as you say and believe. Northrup goes on to say, "You want to know the secret to enduring love? The kind that lights you up inside and attracts a partner? Figure out what fuels your inner fire and stoke it every day. There is nothing sexier, healthier, or more potent than a vital life force." (Northrup, 2014, para. 10) In order for me to find a true relationship, I had to learn to love myself before I could be in a relationship that epitomized true, authentic, genuine, and enduring love.

As of this writing, two of my three children refuse to speak with or visit me. No matter what I do, I get no response. I try calling, visiting, e-mailing, texting, writing, and sending gifts on all of their birthdays. I never know if they get the gifts, as there is not so much as a thank you. I even ask for just a text response of yes or no to indicate that they received their gifts, but to no avail. I cannot imagine the pain they must be feeling.

Through a psychologist friend of mine, I started researching parental alienation syndrome (PAS). This is when children alienate one parent through conscious or subconscious direction from whom psychologists call the aligned parent, the parent that the children identify with as the victim. More often than not, well-adjusted, clear-thinking, and morally developed children of divorce can maintain balance after a reasonable time of disappointment and anger. They can analyze their parents' behavior and the nature of the parent-child relationships, and despite their anger and sadness, stay connected to both parents. They find value in each parent as separate human beings and nurture strong positive memories with each one.

Joan B. Kelly and Janet R. Johnson state in their article *The Alienated Child: A Reformulation of Parental Alienation Syndrome* state that "the core feature of alienation is the extreme disproportion between the child's perception and the beliefs about the rejected parent, and the actual history about the rejected parent's behaviors and the parent-child relationship." (Kelly & Johnson, 2001, p. 262) They are treating the rejected parent as if they never had a positive relationship. The relationship between me and all of my children didn't merit the kind of treatment that I was receiving post-separation. My treatment just doesn't fit the type of relationship we had. That's what made it so puzzling, but yeat again, made me reflect on their pain.

Those who study PAS also warn of retaliatory rejection. My friends warned me of this as well, so I kept trying to stay connected even though the silence and lack of response prevailed. This is to prevent refueling the anger and sense of abandonment that they were feeling. What was interesting was that the aligned parents would insist that they never swayed the children one way or another; they would instead insist that the children made up their own minds about what they wanted to do. These veiled, noncommittal statements from the connected parent that discourage communication with the alienated parent, are usually enough to discourage the alienated parent from reaching out. All of my efforts to communicate with my children were rebuffed, including demands that I never try to contact them again, to stop harassing them with texts, letters, cards, e-mails, visitations, and gifts and cards that were generally left unopened and even discarded.

Once I attempted to visit my daughter at her house and her boyfriend refused to allow me in. After that, my daughter said in an email that if I tried to visit again, she would call the police. This hurt immensely, but that was exactly what she tried to do because she was hurting so much herself. I ask this of people who try to hurt me: What is it about you that is hurting so badly that you want to hurt me? Targeted hate stems from pain and fear. It's not others' actions so much that cause our pain, but our own reaction to the initial action. My initial reaction to my rejection and alienation was to reject and alienate the givers, but I have since realized that this just deepens the pain for all parties concerned. To hate is to maintain connection with the party in question. The opposite of love isn't hate, but indifference and fear. I think at this point in the divorce process I welcomed hate, as it let me know that I was still an object in the lives of my children. Indifference would hurt much more. I feared with time it would come to indifference instead of a healthy healing and a return to love. That's why I found it necessary to maintain contact, and to continue to send love, either real through cards, letters, texts, and phone calls, or telepathically.

My middle child, Mike, (who wanted to stay connected to both parents) warned against this and encouraged that for right now I should give them what they wanted. I was just not sure this was what they wanted. I think they needed to go through the disgust, frustration, hurt, pain, and confusion in order to heal, just as there are phases in death. If I gave them nothing, they would have nothing to use to lash out against me, and they needed that right then.

I think now that Mike was right. I think what my children were asking was that I honor their feelings and not try to run an iron over things by encouraging them to rush through their emotions. I think they wanted to have their moment of hardship so that they had a foundation from which to build a type of deeper character and strength that blossoms and flourishes from adversity. To this point, their lives were pristine, perfect, immaculate, and without flaw. Because of this event, they would become stronger and would grow immensely. I succumbed to these feelings and decided to let them determine when the appropriate time would be for them to reach out with acceptance;

in the meantime, I have found peace with my newfound happiness; content to just send them birthday and holiday greetings.

It was important to me that I had coaching, and that my wife had coaching as well. I needed to be coached to persevere and try to maintain contact as much as possible, at least in the earlier times of the separation. It is my perception that I think my wife needed to be coached to encourage our children to reach out to me and reaccept me into their lives. I felt that if she didn't do this, it would prove in the end to be psychologically damaging to them. The sooner this is done, the better. The longer you wait beyond a reasonable grieving time, the more distant the relationship becomes, which makes it that much harder to heal and reconnect. One must find a balance here between giving enough time to grieve and to heal, and not letting too much time to pass, to prevent distancing and emotional disconnect.

It is said that the alienated parent, especially one with whom the neglect is unjustified, can go into shock and sometimes become depressed, even though the estranged may not have a predisposition to depression. It's one of the hardest things I ever had to go through. Rejection from your own children is unfathomable. I thought I had wonderful individual relationships with all of my children—or at least as good as a father could have. The birthday and Christmas cards from them always had wonderful words of gratitude for who I was and what I had attempted to do for them for all of those years. I had no idea that this was conditional on me staying married or being unhappy in a relationship.

I thought I was an individual. I thought that if anything would ever happen between their mother and me, I would still have been valued as a dad and friend in their adult lives. Why couldn't they see that my detachment wasn't from them? Why couldn't they see that there could still be value in a relationship between their mother and me, which I relayed time and time again? This wonderful woman and I went through a lot together, raised these three wonderful children, and buried people in each other's families. Is what matters here a piece of paper binding two people legally, or what could be realistically salvageable friendship and relationship?

Didn't they understand that there can still be love outside the bonds of marriage? That the love of two people who have been through so much together can enjoy a relationship through an amicable experience? You cannot break the bonds of friendship, siblings, parents, aunts or uncles, or even in-laws that you've created ties with simply by revoking a piece of paper and dividing up some property and a few dollars. Relationships are deeper than this. They are bonds that are experience-based. Marriage is a human-made institution. It's not what connects two people together in God's eyes. What ties two people together are unconditional positive regard, loyalty, friendship, trust, integrity, faith in one another, and reliability. Yes, you can get these things through a legal contract, but it's much more valuable to develop these qualities in a relationship through mutual agreement, as this personal covenant and pact becomes a spiritual agreement that goes way deeper than a written and signed indenture.

What price do we have to pay for falling out of love? For me it was extreme financial loss, but more importantly, the loss of my children. What goes through spouses' minds when asked for a separation or divorce? Do they think of revenge first? Is it comparable to murder, rape, violence, or any other felony? Is falling out of love an act that deserves revenge? Isn't the person who falls out of love a victim here as well? I wanted nothing more than to remain in love with my wife and be happy for the last twenty or thirty years of my life with her as we watched our children continue to grow and develop as mature adults. So it was disappointing to me as well for the last ten years to realize that I was in a loveless marriage, feeling empty, alone, and incapable of loving this woman I married.

What is the alternative here? Do we continue to live in a loveless relationship going through meaningless motions? Do we do this so that we won't fall victim to extreme financial loss? Do we endure so that our children won't be angry and upset with us? Do we practice tolerance so we don't disappoint our relatives and friends, or from the fear of being outcasts? I feel that it is imperative that we step outside of ourselves and take a long look at the physical and spiritual being that inhabits our bodies and admire the gift of this life that God has given us and that we treat this person as generously and as lovingly as we do others. To disregard ourselves as deserving creatures is to reject this gift from our source and to isolate ourselves from the wholeness and collective consciousness that make us all one.

Chapter 8

Conflict Resolution

I believe that the basic nature of human beings is gentle and compassionate. It is therefore in our own interest to encourage that nature, to make it live within us, to leave room for it to develop. If on the contrary we use violence, it is as if we voluntarily obstruct the positive side of human nature and prevent its evolution.

—His Holiness the Dalai Lama

One might ask why I am including conflict resolution in this manuscript, but I feel it is the lifeblood of our very coexistence with others. Whenever there are at least two minds, two personalities, two sets of beliefs, and two sets of desires, wants, and needs, there is conflict. If implemented correctly, conflict is a good thing. It is a way of navigating between our own desires and the desires and needs of an organization or institution, and working within the confines of others' needs and desires. We don't live in a vacuum, but coexist in a world where couples or groups interact to accomplish tasks for the better good of ourselves and others.

Politics Trumps Accomplishments

It is often said that the two most important things in life are the people you love and the work that you do. We spend one third of our lives at work, and if we're lucky, we enjoy it most of the time. Except for a few odd jobs out of high school here and there, I can honestly say that I have truly enjoyed my work. I spent the first half of my working life as an electrical craftsman—installing, troubleshooting, and construction. Every day was a different experience. What's interesting is you spend half the time on conceptual thinking and the other half on implementing those thoughts. When you tell people that you are in some type of craft, they often respond that it's nice that you work with your hands. I have never seen, in fact, a manipulative skill that didn't require thought first.

This type of attitude toward trade skills could end up being dangerous to those who feel that they can do these things without much thought. Even with a lot of thought, inevitable mistakes occur. Skilled people's lives have been lost or serious injuries occur during construction because of miscalculations and errors made by the best of them. For the most part, however, trained craftsmen, who regularly include safety as part of their everyday routine, can enjoy a long and illustrious career, and there's nothing quite like the enjoyment and satisfaction of seeing a task or job come to completion. Ironworkers who have just finished a high-rise skeletal structure often place an evergreen tree and an American flag on top. The evergreen signifies that no one was killed during the process, and the flag, of course, represents American labor at work. I still get great satisfaction installing an outlet or an electrical appliance and feel a sense of accomplishment. Because of the skill set required, I am able to install something that others will use with confidence and have faith that it was installed correctly and safely. There's always a sense of pride and satisfaction in this.

So what makes working in a craft not as fun as it should be is what occurs in every profession, and that's the human contact that inevitably draws out conflict with others. You could have the most pleasant working conditions and still not be happy because others sometimes can make conditions pleasant or unpleasant if you let them. It could be that mean boss or that obnoxious coworker. Most often it is a clique of people that make you feel isolated and alienated. This often occurs in childhood, and one might not expect it in the work world among adults, but it's alive and well. Everyone has a horror story about different people that they worked with, and you often hear the phrase that "I like the work I do; I just don't like the people I work with." The only solution is to make the best of your work environment by using conflict-resolution skills.

David Augsberger, in his book *Caring Enough to Confront,* presents an abundance of skills, techniques, and procedures to approach conflict resolution. Augsberger speaks of care-fronting: "Care-fronting is a loving and level conversation. It unites the love one has for the other with the honest truth that you are able to see about the two of you." (Augsberger, 2009, p. 10) Many of us at one time or another have resorted to silent withdrawal. Others resort to explosive counterattacks. Both are self-defeating; what you need are clear, nondestructive statements about your wants, needs, and feelings. If I confront about what I really want or need, I am caring enough about the relationship with those with whom I am conflicted. Both parties obviously have to agree to confront on an adult and mature level.

I was recently employed by a school district and unknowingly placed into a political hotbed within a contentious and hostile office culture. The position was for a high school principal, and it turned out that the current acting principal, who had the position for the four previous years as an interim principal, was being replaced. This was problematic in itself, but what intensified the problem was that they kept the assistant principal (former acting principal) in the same building as myself. This person had a gender-discrimination lawsuit pending, and the superintendent and board members feared this. In my estimation, the person seeking the lawsuit instilled fear in her supervisors, which in effect already made her the victor of the suit.

The working relationship was doomed from the start. I was willing to work as a team and share the responsibilities, but the newly appointed assistant was not. The school board, which was divided on this issue, maintained division even after the vote was cast. The board members who were not in favor of the change found ways to harass and intimidate me. Their hope was they would find something they could use to fire me, or that I would get disgusted and quit. The school board members who were in my corner were very supportive but could not stop this political harassment. To make things worse, the superintendent of schools favored this newly appointed assistant principal as well, and whenever I instituted an idea or directive, the assistant would go to the superintendent and have my directive overturned. I felt isolated, abandoned, and powerless, but managed to stay in this job for a year before I began seriously looking for another leadership position elsewhere.

All of my diversified experience meant nothing here. I was an intruder. The assistant principal built a nice rapport with the students and the teachers over the last four years, so I really didn't have their support either. The board took another vote after the vote to bring me on board, which was whether to inform me of the dark political climate I was about to enter or to keep me in the dark. They voted not to tell me because they felt if I knew the situation upon which I was about to embark, I would have opted not to take the position. They were probably right, but when the board president told me of this vote to keep me alienated from the knowledge of the situation, I was furious. I had no opportunity for a defense, so went into this position as if I were an accepted leader in this school. It wasn't until after a few incidences that I began to realize what was occurring.

Also, there were a few dissidents on the staff who did not like the assistant principal. It's not that these people were supportive of me; it was that I may have represented someone who was opposed to the incumbent. I don't really care for this type of support and let it be known. One could tell it was not genuine because it was immediate and always led to discussions about what the assistant principal did wrong and how unfairly this person treated people. In fact, this person actually did a fine job. I never had an issue with this person. It was the school board's and the superintendent's decisions that eventually set up an environment of division and chaos.

One such incident involved one of the secretaries taking a photograph of me while I was on my cell phone during my lunch hour. One of the dissidents informed me that this happened, so I brought the perpetrator into my office and let her know that I felt that it was a violation of my civil rights and I reported her to the superintendent. The superintendent ran an iron over it and we moved forward. From this incident on, there seemed to be a concerted effort to sabotage my tenure through being undermined, spied on, and harassed. There was an effort to defame my character, both professionally and personally, in order to coerce me to quit.

So how did I handle all of this? From the practicality side of things and taking into consideration that I was getting paid handsomely biweekly, I wasn't worried. There were two driving forces in me, however, that would not allow this simple complacency to continue. One, I am by nature a change agent, always wanting to improve what I feel are targeted weaknesses; and two, I felt like I wasn't earning my salary. Since the assistant principal still wanted to run the school, I was left only to work with outside influences in the business and industry community. Although this was an integral part of my job description, it only takes a little time to manage this, and for the most part I was bored and always trying to create my own work without disturbing the school operations already being handled. I never challenged the assistant, as I felt this was not this person's doing. I always tried to maintain a professional balance and rapport and just tried to work on non-conflicting projects. These, too, were challenged at times, but I managed to remain the bigger person. I felt at this point that since I was aggressively looking for other employment opportunities, it was not necessary to stir things up any more than they already were.

The school district where I had become employed had its share of serious issues and weaknesses, and I soon learned that I alone could not invoke enough change to make a difference. It's difficult sometimes to sit back and watch these injustices, knowing that in the end, the schoolchildren are the ones who are shortchanged. The climate in this district implied that the "kids come first and we need to do what benefits the students," but the culture indicated otherwise. It was the personal advancement of the employees and the nepotism that really underpinned the foundation of the culture there. I have learned, however, to challenge those things that can be changed because confrontation is necessary for growth. Confrontation should and must be employed in a correct manner to invoke change, and it must be understood by those that are led.

Augsberger states, "When unchallenged, human beings often become self-centered, individualistic, and self-absorbed. When unchallenged, human groups tend to drift, wander, or stagnate. When unchallenged, relationships tend to repeat, become routine, become stale, or stuck. Life, without challenge or confrontation is directionless, aimless, passive; or selfish, self-serving, empty. Confrontation, uncomfortable as it can be, is a gift." (Augsberger, 2009, p. 61)

Confrontation, when done correctly, comes from love. It is well-intentioned, and the consummate leader knows how to use confrontation in a caring and compassionate manner to evoke change necessary for a person, group, or relationship to grow and flourish.

Chapter 9

Education

How many a man has dated a new era in his life from
the reading of a book! The book exists for us, perchance,
that will explain our miracles and reveal new ones.

—Henry David Thoreau

When I was in third grade, our long-term project assignment was to make our mothers a jewelry box out of cigar boxes, which were very popular at the time because, of course, more men smoked back then. When the teacher introduced the project, she made them look so beautiful. Some were painted black and decorated with sequins with sparkling colored glitter on them. She told us the best place to get them was in a drugstore, as they sold individual cigars right out of the box and the box would become available when empty. I had no luck. My mother and I went to our local drugstore and they had none, but they said to check back in a week or so and maybe one would be available. None were available then or even the week after. I guess my mother wasn't resourceful enough, and I certainly wasn't so I was never able to obtain one.

There were times during the week when the teacher said in transition that we were allowed to get our boxes out and work on them for a period. At the elementary level, we had one teacher for all subjects, so we transitioned into art and music quite frequently. I used to dread when she made the announcement, as I was the only student who didn't have a box. When everyone was working on theirs, I would just stand at my desk and watch the other students work on them. Some students would remind me that I didn't have a box (as if I didn't know) and kept on working.

I thought I was fooling the teacher, but as I look back, I can't imagine a teacher not knowing that one of her students was not participating in the project, so I often wonder what she was thinking or why she lacked the motivation to help me succeed. I as a teacher would have gone out and found a box somewhere or even made one out of cardboard or wood.

When I could see the project was winding down around the Christmas holiday and most students were finishing up, I felt a sense of relief that I wouldn't have to fake participation anymore. To my chagrin, however, the teacher called each student up one at a time to grade the project; I remember being so nervous and anxious about what I was going to do or say when she called my name. When she finally did, I went up empty-handed, and she asked where my box was. When I said I didn't have one, her response was simply, "That's easy; you get an F," and she proceeded to call the next name on the list.

First of all, what was she grading—students' art ability, completion time, neatness, creativity? These were third graders that were making a gift for their moms. Was there no assessment of the process, the effort of being on task, or even the collaborative work that some of the students were doing? Was this simply a period off for this teacher, who was totally oblivious that one of her students was not able to participate? Did she leave a child behind in her apathy and indifference?

I never forgot that experience, but it helped me as a teacher because I always knew what each and every one of my students were doing and what they needed and wanted, and I offered praise and constructive criticism along the way. I treated them equally, regardless of their ability to provide some of their own materials, their academic abilities, shortcomings, disabilities, and attitudes. I loved unconditionally. I was able to take my guilt and shame and turn it into a constructive approach to my teaching.

It's funny that no matter how young we were, we were able to decipher what we would do differently if we were the teacher. Maybe we should be asking these questions of our third graders. If you were the teacher, what would you do differently? What teacher action or verbiage made you feel good about yourself; badly about yourself? Teachers get upset about the idea of having students fill out course surveys at the end of the school year, as they feel that they are getting evaluated by their students. A strong teacher wouldn't mind this because, for the most part, he or she would be pretty confident that the surveys would be positive. This is because strong teachers know how to build relationships with their students.

The most important aspect about what makes a good school is not the latest technology, equipment, or facility, but the relationships the teachers foster with their students. There are very few relationships as sacred as a student-teacher relationship because, in reality, sometimes the teacher is the student and the student is the teacher. In many cases, the students spend more time in the course of the day with their teachers than they do with their parents.

When I walked up to the counter at the bookstore at the community college that I attended, I felt apprehensive and reluctant to place my order for my books, as I had no cash with me. Because of my father's death, I was eligible for social security benefits until I was twenty-one, so I had asked the student-clerk behind the counter if my social security benefits would pay for the books. I had come from a high school environment where everyone knew everything about me, so I assumed that my records would show that my books would be covered. I was so naïve and was very embarrassed, although the student-clerk behind the counter was very nice.

Although I didn't fare well at Bucks County Community College, I loved it there. Since ivy was indigenous to the area, the older buildings had it growing all over the sides. There were sprawling beautiful flower gardens with fountains and sculptures. The land and buildings were donated by the Tyler family of Chestnut Hill, Pennsylvania. They loved art, particularly sculpture, and there were awesome sculptures all over the campus. When I took the required music classes in Tyler Hall in the fall of my freshman year, I used to stare out of the window at the falling colorful leaves while listening to symphonies. Although I remember musical genres such as sonatas and recitatives that were mentioned by our professor, I didn't commit them much to memory, so therefore did not do well on his exams.

I don't think it was a bad thing, however, to sit there and take in the beautiful music and scenery and actually live in the moment. Imagine the professor saying, "All right, your assignment for today is to focus on the landscaping outside of the window while listening to Beethoven's Fifth, and then write a one-page summary on what went through your head as you participated in this activity and share it with the rest of the class." In essence, you would be sharing with the class and the professor your true appreciation of the art that surrounded you.

English composition was my favorite class, as I loved to write even back then. I've been told many times in my life by many people, including college professors, that I should pursue writing as a career. I didn't have a strong math background in high school, so didn't fare well in that subject either.

In my second year at Bucks, I took a speech class. I found the professor to be very arrogant. We had to do a persuasive speech, and mine was on birth control using the rhythm method, as that's what the Catholic Church was a proponent of. Any type of birth control that was not natural or required some sort of drug was frowned upon. At one point in the speech, I had my classmates laughing when I jokingly stated that if you had relations that day without considering the rhythm method, you had better go out and purchase a box of pampers if you happened to just kiss your wife good-bye as you left for work. Anyway, it was well-received by my classmates, but I was only given a C grade by the professor. I pleaded and challenged this grade, but he refused to change the grade. He explained, "You should not bring the Catholic religion into your speeches." I tried to explain that it wasn't the content that should be graded in a speech class, but the delivery and style and if I were persuasive or not. All to no avail, and I stormed out of the class and never went back.

I received a D for the class and ended up having to take speech class over at Temple University in order to graduate because Ds are not transferable. There was no way I was going to change that teacher's mind, but I learned a very valuable lesson here. Wayne Dyer, in his book *I Can See Clearly Now*, says that when given a choice to be right or kind, always choose kind. He shares this in a story about challenging one of his college professor's decisions on giving him a bad grade on a report on an article that he wrote. The grade never changed, but there was a valuable lesson to be learned here about righteousness and kindness. When he received that poor grade on a writing assignment that required him to reflect on a particular author's writing, he sent his paper to the author. The author praised him for his work and stated that Dr. Dyer's reflection was exactly correct. Again, this made no difference to the professor and in the end, Dr. Dyer realized that being right made no difference. He should have been kind and accepted his professor's critique. In the end, I felt like I lost the opportunity for a unique teacher-student relationship and perhaps burned a bridge. It made no difference in my professional life or the professor's for that matter but an opportunity for a valuable human connection was lost and it has been my experience that the loss of relationship stays with you longer than what grade you received on an assignment, a job interview that you felt you did well on but didn't get, or an award that went to someone else that you felt you deserved.

I attended most of Temple University part-time in the evenings and during the summers and was able to complete my degree there. Temple has a lovely campus situated on the north side of Philadelphia on Broad Street. Most of the classes were large and not personal, but I was okay with this. Some of the summer classes were smaller, however, and it was nice to become friends with other part-time students and bounce ideas and information off them.

I received my master's degree from Chestnut Hill College in Philadelphia, which is another beautiful old school. My major was applied technology in education, and I hit it at exactly the right time, as PowerPoint was just coming out along with Adobe Premiere; they were both considered great technology tools to use. I'll never forget Sister Loraine, the head of the applied technology program; I would have never expected her to be so technologically savvy, but she fooled me. She was the kindest and most wonderful woman and nun you'd ever want to meet. I wanted to leave the program a few times because I felt it was too rigid, but she convinced me to stay.

One particular female professor seemed like she did everything she could to prevent me from graduating. She seemed okay until she found out that I was teaching in a vocational setting, and she wasn't shy about letting me know that I really didn't belong in this prestigious college. The fact is my Miller Analogy scores were off the charts, so the fact that I got in should have been enough to convince her that I was capable of the work. There was also a self-proclaimed-flamboyant gay man in our class whom she seemed to favor. In my eyes it was a blatant case of exploitation of this young man—sort of like saying, "Everyone, look at me; I'm forward-thinking as I have befriended a gay man."

It reminded me of the time at my son's first soccer game of the season when there were new teams and parents didn't know each other yet. There were about six fathers standing there, one of whom was an African American man. Another father approached the group and singled out the African American man, vociferously greeting him and shaking his hand. After that, he walked away from the group, greeting no one else. He was showboating and exploited this man to say, "I am a progressive thinker." What he was really saying was, "I'll use this African American man to make myself look good in front of all of these parents."

Anyway, I ended up graduating from the program despite this professor's arrogance. It's terrible to say, but I remember her so well, and remember very little about the other professors, who were equitable and treated everyone with fairness and kindness. I guess sometimes it's human nature to remember the worst experiences, and this could be by design. I believe we grow and learn better from our worst experiences so we make sure that we handle things differently the next time. I wasn't going to change that teacher; I could only change myself. From then on I learned to accept and tolerate those with whom we struggle and keep focused on the people who educate us using positive methods of communication and teaching.

I'll never forget the pain I suffered one horrible night. My whole chest and abdomen were pounding and ached like nothing I had ever felt before. My head was throbbing and I felt dizzy. It was about midnight, and just then my wife came in from her second shift at the hospital. She called 911, and the ambulance came to take me to the hospital where my wife had just come from. I was sure it was a massive heart attack, and I think the paramedics felt the same way. One of the paramedics proceeded to put a nitro tablet under my tongue and then made me take a couple of aspirin. That was all I needed to feel like I was going to projectile vomit all over the place. Luckily they had the bags, and I think I filled two of them. I seemed to then get a little relief, but wasn't sure if it was from the vomiting or from the nitro tablet I ingested. It turns out it wasn't a heart attack, but a severe case of pancreatitis. My gall bladder, as it turned out, was sludgy from over the years and had a negative impact on my pancreas.

After an eleven-day hospital stay full of flushing and starvation and the removal of my gall bladder, I began to feel myself again, but had a long road to recovery. What does this have to do with my education? I have attributed this to pursuing my doctoral degree and writing my dissertation. I don't know if there are any studies done on this, but I've heard it is not unusual for your body to crash like this after the grueling work of getting a PhD.

I attended Penn State University for this program, and it was about three and a half hours away from my home. I was fortunate to take some courses online and some weeklong courses in the summer, but still had to take a few courses that met once a week. The commute was brutal, and I had to make it up and back in the same day. I left at two o'clock for a six o'clock class and left class at nine o'clock and would arrive home at midnight. I found out which professors were more lenient about cutting class and chose a lot of those courses, but for the most part attended religiously. The courses were interesting, and I managed to muddle through.

I wrote my dissertation after my course work was complete. I'll never forget my defense. By the time the panel was through with me and asked me to leave the room so they could deliberate, I was sure I had failed. I couldn't imagine being beaten up like that and not failing. When I returned to the room, they shook my hand and congratulated me. I was stunned. Contingent on some revisions, I passed. How does a person feel who actually fails?

A couple of weeks later, I fell victim to this pancreatitis thing. I believe this was something that would have happened sooner or later but was precipitated by the PSU experience. Being called doctor is nice, but I always thought this should be preserved for medical doctors. I thought that professor or something else would be more fitting. When someone calls out Dr. Viviano, I still look around for perhaps a more imposing figure. I often look back and ask why I put myself through that. Was it an overachieving syndrome because I came from an economically disadvantaged environment, was it because my father uttered those words that I would be the first person in my family to go to college, or was it simply wanting to grow? My brother-in-law Jack, from my former marriage and a PhD himself, calls me the poster child for growth. Some of what he says about me inspired me to write this book, as I have always admired him.

Education, particularly career and technical education, has been and continues to be my life. I firmly believe that all of us should start out sweeping floors and then exercising the prophecy that education is lifelong. When we are young and strong, we should use our bodies more than our minds to build something from another's ideas; and as we age, we become the idea makers and pass the labor on down to our youth, who are strong and have great follow-ship skills.

Chapter 10

A Word from
My Parents

I first found out I was psychic next Tuesday.

—Unknown

wasn't there to protect you, Tommy. I didn't know how. In fact, you protected me. That night when the strangers were walking up the basement steps, I was scared—scared for you, scared for me. (As I think of this I reflect on Wayne Dyer's quote from the *Course in Miracles* that there are only two types of emotions that we have inside: fear and love. And where there is fear, no love can be found; and where there is love, there is no fear.) I loved you and still do, but the fear inside me didn't let me show that and prevented me from protecting you as a mother should from the bullies, from the cruel teachers, from poverty, and sometimes even from your father, who loved you very much but only did as a father what he learned as a son.

You have such a big heart, Tommy, and I am so proud of you. Because of your childhood, you put up many walls and shields, and they are still with you today. They are a huge fortress that block out all the happiness you could hope to have. You are guarded and fortified, and until recently, nothing and no one could possibly penetrate your defenses. Take down this shield and open up to the universe that loves you. You have begun to do this with a journal that your best friend has given you. Yes, I read what you wrote, Tommy.

"Mom, thank you for everything you tried to do for me. I know now that you did the best that you could for me and the girls, and I now realize how hard this could have been for you. I know you are here now. I know you would be proud of my family, the friendships I have cultivated, and the work that I do. I am sorry that we didn't have a better relationship. I guess things are just what they are meant to be. I'm sure we'll be together again someday."

And that we will, Tommy. You will love this spiritual world. When we leave our bodies, we continue to grow and learn, and it would take an infinitive amount of time to learn everything there is to know about our existence, universal love, spirituality, and self-actualization. But that's the fun of it all. It's a miracle every time you discover something new. You have it right, Tommy, as you seem to want to absorb all the information you can while in your physical form. Your solid form allows you to touch others physically, and the power of touch is so underrated. Your body is a vehicle and conduit for your feeling to flow through. Continue to learn all you can.

You survived adversity for a reason, and that's to teach. Teach others that they are not alone, that they are all geniuses, and that they just have to believe in themselves and the unlimited potential that they have in becoming spiritual and wondrous human beings. Teach them that their adversities can be overcome, and that they in turn can help others overcome. Adversity is good, as it makes us who we are. There can be no growth without it, and you cannot be shielded from it. Here I reflect on Elisabeth Kubler-Ross when she says, "Should you shield the canyon from the windstorm, you would never see the beauty of the carvings." (iz Quotes website, 2014, p. 1)

It is your dad, Tommy. I am surprised that I come to you through this medium wanting to speak what is in my heart because I could never do this before when I was with you. I am so proud of you. You are able to say what is in your heart. Out of love and caring, I may have abused you somewhat as a child. I used straps and sticks to make you change your behavior. I may not have bruised you or broken anything, but I think I may have broken your spirit. I may have put the fear of God into you and left you unable and unwilling to express yourself as you should.

This has impacted you throughout the years after my passing, and for this, I cannot say enough how sorry I am. The very one who should have protected you hurt you instead, and you felt betrayed, sometimes even unloved. But I assure you, Tommy, that nothing is further from the truth. I loved you deeply, and I raised you how I was raised. I wish it could have been different. I wish I could have broken the cycle. You did, Tommy, with your children. You got it right. Your children grew up with the safety and freedom to speak their minds and to be true to themselves.

I received the words from your journal. "Dad, to this day I miss you terribly. I wish you could meet my family, my friends, the people that I love, and I wish they could get to know the wonderful person that you are. You would be so proud of my son Tommy, who is an ordained priest in the archdiocese of Philadelphia. I remember how spiritual you were and dedicated to God and Jesus Christ. You would be so proud of Mike, who is so intelligent and thinks globally and outside of the box. And of Christina, who is so beautiful, so grounded, and I'm sure you would fall in love with her if you met her. You would have been appreciative of my ex-wife, who took over as my protector when you could not be there anymore. And you would love Lisa, who is another guiding light in my life. I am sorry that I was a difficult son at times. I love and miss you. Tommy."

Write your book, son. It will help you tear down the walls that shield your heart from the people that you love, and who love you. Open up to these people, and to all of the people who will read your book, for you have much to teach, much to learn, and much to share. You are an inspiration and a very special person. You have a big heart; you are a giver, a server, and a healer. This is your dharma, your purpose, your reason for occupying your physical form. Let people in, and let go. I'm glad you kept all of the good that I left within you: to be respectful of people but stand up for yourself when you have to.

And the music, Tommy, as I can hear you play and sing, and the angels that surround you love it too. Music is a conduit to the heart. Don't worry too much about what you do with religion, but always be spiritual. We will be together someday, and you're going to love it here. You pick up where you left off as a physical being and continue to learn, grow, teach, heal, and guard. You are right in trying to learn all you can as a physical being because this phase of your life has connections to your previous spiritual existence and onto the next.

Our physical being is an essential part of our overall spiritual growth, as there are things you can do with a physical body that you are unable to do without it. The privilege of touch can only be achieved through physical existence and is an extremely powerful act. We don't forget those physical acts when we cross over, so they serve to reinforce our emotional and intellectual growth. Take every opportunity to touch other humans in chorus with vocal expressions of adoration and regard. Fill all of your senses with their essence of being so you take with you fond remembrance of how they touched your life.

Chapter 11

A Word about Love

Being deeply loved by someone gives you strength, while loving someone deeply gives you courage. Kindness in words creates confidence. Kindness in thinking creates profoundness. Kindness in giving creates love. Because of a great love, one is courageous. Love is of all passions the strongest, for it attacks simultaneously the head, the heart and the senses.

—The Tao

These are very powerful and impactful words. This is how I feel of one whom I love and who loves me. I feel that her love for me gives me strength, and I have become more courageous in loving her. Our kindness in words and actions toward one another gives us both confidence and a better understanding of who we are and what we deserve. The kindness in our acceptance of each other's thoughts allows for an outlet in which to express creative and profound points of view. And the kindness expressed by what we give each other nurtures our love for one another.

I feel her love in all of my senses, even extended sixth senses like emotion and humility. It allows me to explore and examine emotional and mindful territories where I have never gone before—previously averted because of an unrealistic fear of something. In a sense, we have opened our worlds up to a vulnerability that neither of us has experienced before because of fortresses we may have set up to prevent us from getting hurt. Maybe we shielded ourselves from harm in the safety of our abodes. Since we released ourselves from the confines of our bastion, we can now soar to new plateaus and levels never experienced before. And this type of emancipation feels wonderful, for the only roadblocks that we now experience would be the ones that we erect ourselves.

I hope this all makes sense to you, because it does to me. People go through their whole lives and don't experience this. This is sad, as I wish everyone would have what we have. I don't think it's a weakness to need someone else. It is said that we need to love ourselves before we can love and be loved by others. This is probably true to a point, but that's not to say we should not search for and nurture that mate who can help us define and identify ourselves—the real us, not the us that we created and invented to protect us from whatever it was that we were afraid of. Sometimes we need that sounding board or mirror to reflect back at us who we are, what we want and need, and help us to bring out the best in us to be all that we can be.

It is said that the intelligence of a group (couple) is larger than the individual intelligences of each participant. I believe this to be true of emotional depth as well. The emotional depth of a group (couple) is larger than the sum of the individual emotional depths. It doesn't always have to be a romantic partner. It can be a friend, a relative, or a therapist that can guide us into our internal path for happiness. Our souls in isolation have no purpose, but when shared, open up a world of endless possibilities to help others learn, grow, develop, share, and impact all of those that come into contact with us.

Love is contagious, and when people in love are around others, the others can feel the love, and something happens chemically inside to help us live better and longer. Love all that you can. It costs nothing, and the rewards are boundless.

References

Augsberger, D. (2009). *Caring enough to confront*. Ventura, CA: Regal.

Benard, B. (1995). *Fostering resilience in children*. Retrieved from http:// resilnet.uiuc.edu/library/benard95.html

Brown, B. (June, 2010, June, 2010). *The power of vulnerability* [Video file]. Retrieved from http://www.ted.com/talks/brene_brown_on_ vulnerability

Dyer, W. W. (2007). *Change your thoughts—change your life: Living the wisdom of the Tao*. Carlsbad, CA: Hay House.

Dyer, W. W. (2014). *I can see clearly now*. Carlsbad, CA: Hay House.

Houston, J. (2012). *The wizard of us*. New York: Atria Books.

Kelly, J. B., & Johnson, J. R. (2001). The alienated child: A reformulation of parental alienated syndrome. Retrieved from http://onlinelibrary. wiley.com/doi/10.1111/j.174-1617.2001.tb00609.x/abstract

Northrup, C. (2014). Christiane northrup. Retrieved from http:// themainemag.com/people/profiles/1603-dr-christiane-northrup.html

Sennett, R. (2008). *The craftsman*. New York: Yale University Press.

Singer, M. A. (2007). *The untethered soul*. Oakland, CA: New Harbinger Publications.

iz Quotes website. (2014). http://izquotes.com/quote/105641